Living Well While Doing Good

OTHER BOOKS BY DONNA SCHAPER

Grassroots Gardening: Rituals for Sustaining Activism
On Tiptoes in Expectation: Prayers for Advent,
Christmas, and Epiphany
Labyrinths from the Outside In
The Art of Spiritual Rock Gardening
Sacred Speech
Mature Grief: When a Parent Dies
Sabbath Sense
Sabbath Keeping

LIVING WELL WHILE DOING GOOD

DONNA SCHAPER

SEABURY BOOKS
an imprint of Church Publishing, Inc., New York

v

Library of Congress Cataloging-in-Publication Data
Schaper, Donna.
  Living well while doing good / Donna Schaper.
      p.   cm.
  ISBN 978-1-59627-047-3 (pbk.)
  1. Conduct of life. 2. Simplicity—Religious aspects—
Christianity. 3. Schaper, Donna. I. Title.

BJ1521.S33 2007
241—dc22

                              2007005351

Printed in the United States of America.

Church Publishing, Incorporated
445 Fifth Avenue
New York, New York 10016
www.churchpublishing.org

5   4   3   2   1

For Warren,
my partner of twenty-five years,
who does good and helps me live well

 CONTENTS

 INTRODUCTION

A GOOD LIGHT

This book began in a hard decision I had to make. I loved my position as head pastor of a South Florida church, where I had been for a short four years. The last job my husband could have gotten at a local university was given to someone else, so he had commuted for four years from Hartford to Miami and looked at every single academic opening. As chair of the history department at the University of Hartford, he really didn't want to give up tenure or risk working outside its protection. While I wanted to stay, I also did not want him to continue what had turned into a brutal commute. Nor did I want to live alone on a permanent basis, with commuting as a permanent lifestyle. While we had been happily married for twenty-two years, able to live well and do good for twenty-plus years, we were at the end of our good luck.

Complicating my every effort to make a decision about what to do was the sheer pressure of time. The decision knotted up into a ball of string even a kitten could not unravel. This issue tied up with that issue, which made a coalition with another issue. Feminism quarreled with family, then family with feminism. I was damned if I was going

1

to be a woman who broke the stained-glass ceiling—and then gave it up for family. I also couldn't do the job alone; I needed the support of my partner. I finally admitted that I had no time in which to pull the strings apart and see what I needed to do.

Far from keeping a regular Sabbath, I was working all the time, rushing to save the city of Miami from doing one stupid thing or another. Everything outside seemed to be more important than what was inside me—which was a growing confusion and fatigue. The poor and unemployed were always part of the web: how dare I fret about the plenty of my life and its double binds when the worst thing that could happen to me is I could return to the farm on which we raised our children up north? We hadn't sold the house. I wasn't going to starve. I would surely find more work. My plenty, compared to the world's poverty, mocked the fact that I had no time even to make a decision about how to distribute my plenty.

If during this period of *wazu wazu*, as a Liberian friend of mine calls personal chaos, I had had a regular day off— even if not a worshiping day—I would have been able to slide into a decision. Instead I literally had to pull myself away for a week and go on personal retreat to do remedial work in Sabbath-keeping. By Sabbath I mean nothing more or less than time for *being* rather than *doing*. What I learned in my make-up week was not pretty: I had become one of those activists I cannot abide. Without me, all of Miami's movements were going to crumble. Children would starve. Meetings would be mishandled. The wrong people would be elected. Atlas had the world firmly placed on her shoulders, so important to her schemes of social change that she had begun to do violence to the very movements she promoted. No longer an attractive advocate, instead she was burned-out.

Imagine how bad it would be if a new grant for our microlending program might not get written! I had to face into my overdoneness. I had been baked too long in my legitimate activist hopes and lost the sense of balance and humor that were my only way of negotiating my work/family conflict. Where had it gone? It had gone to overwork, conceit, indispensability, and the other usual traits of ineffective activists. When things come to be "all up to us," an insidious dependency has tied us up in knots. We are the prisoners, not the servants, of our activism.

Oddly, I should have known. I have written several books on Sabbath-keeping and more often than not, find a way to keep a Sabbath. But now I used my "usefulness" to the world as a way to protect myself from the pain of life direction. I joined activists of many ilks and worlds: I avoided my own life and its authority on behalf of "others."

At such times my light goes out. I can't even keep a little fire burning, much less achieve my grandiose objectives. Busyness and hyperactivity are a way to jiggle the key in the doors of my prison, but they won't work to get me out. Activists, more than any others, need time to be as well as do. The very doing of activists is prejudiced by its lack of balance. Activists who do not know how many touches, hits, meetings, phone calls, and issues are *enough* is violating Sabbath. They are abusing time by overusing it. Rules number one, two, and three for activists are defining, personally, what constitutes *enough*. Many others will be happy to define *enough* for you. Their measure for your life will always be too much. *Enough* is yours to define. It holds the key to living well while doing good. Activists who refrain from self- and job-definition are in constant danger of violating the nature of time and acting without limits in a world of limits. A better definition of idolatry I cannot imagine. We substitute our limited fantasy of limitlessness for the actual limitlessness of God.

Instead of picking up ten twigs and making a small fire, we pick up more than we can handle. We then proceed to drop and scatter them. Instead of keeping a good light, we keep no light at all.

I was a danger to myself and others. Many activists make this mistake with time. We assume we are better than the average working Joe. Just because they are captive to their bosses about time doesn't mean we are. Even if we haven't had dinner with our families for weeks, so what? We are doing the work of God, the work of the movements. We buy into a dangerous holier-than-thou. From there the social change we effect hurts the genuinely put-down as much as it helps them.

What finally saved me was a walk in a labyrinth in the woods at Kirkridge, a retreat center outside of Stroudsburg, Pennsylvania, where I had been many times. In its centered peace I needed to empty myself, to pour out all the self-serving myths about my utter indispensability. After about four days of hiking around on the Appalachian Trail in relatively desultory fashion, almost as though the back-and-forth were the pattern of my decision-making paralysis, I fell into a deep sleep. I woke the next morning to all but rush out of the cabin around 6 A.M. I went straight to the labyrinth and said that I would walk in. At the center, I would know which choice I was making. I would then walk out loving the choice I had made. To stay in Florida would have been fine; to leave Florida would also be fine. The time had come to decide. I had no idea what the decision would be. Instead I knew there would be a decision, that wonderful word that comes from *de cidere,* which has the verb "to kill" as its root. I was going to kill one of the two possibilities for my life.

I got to the center of the labyrinth. There was a rock. I sat on it for what seemed a long time but what was actually a short time. The rock said, you are going back to Amherst. You are ending the commute. I said fine. I then walked out of the circle of circles with a joy and lightness I can't remember ever experiencing before. Something had died.

Something was born. I had walked into it; now I was walking out of it.

The Sabbath had given me the rest to know what I should do. The labyrinth was just the pattern of unraveling the yarns that had been all balled up. The yarns were simply a messy version of the labyrinth. They mirrored each other—one in its confusion, the other in its simplicity. What made the difference? Why did this labyrinth break through in decision on this day? Who knows! The labyrinth can't be used as a gimmick. It works when it will and it doesn't work when it won't, and that is all there is to it. It gives us a picture of life that quarrels with the knotted-up one. That helps. What appears to be true in using the labyrinth to make decisions is that we let the circles take care of us. We give ourselves up to them and they repattern us.

I knew I had to find a method to get through. I had to draw a line in the sand. I needed to give up being so damn important on behalf of finding my way forward. Otherwise I was just walking in circles. Because of this trip to the labyrinth, I walked out in peace. Without the Sabbath, without taking the time off and finding my own center, I would have remained paralyzed. From time to time I would have lucked into doing something worthwhile for someone else. But finally my embers were going out. I was unsustainable. I had fallen off my high wire and was more a part of people's despair than of their hope. Because I chose to live well, both by making a decision and disappointing my ambitions, I returned to a simpler fire. I also created the possibility of lighting another fire elsewhere, of keeping a good light longer.

 CHAPTER ONE

SIMPLIFYING FIRES

L iving well while doing good is first of all an interpretive art in which we think, and then act. Both the living well and the doing good are one action richly connected, like a labyrinth—inseparable, married, in deep fear of divorce or estrangement. Inner needs outer the way outer needs inner. When third-world activists speak of "decolonizing the imagination first," they teach us to take control of our own lives and our own definitions and our own numbers. We are to measure ourselves. We are to evict the colonizers, whom action activists think of as "external" but which are also "internal." We both take control of ourselves and release control of ourselves; like the labyrinth, they are one action. We measure what little we may dare call success in changing the world, and then we let the rest go. We walk into action and we walk out from action into being.

The key strategy to living well while doing good is to simplify. I call the strategy "simplifiers," using a play on words. We make "simple fires"—we tame our passions. We have simultaneous light and warmth. We measure how much of a blaze we need. Many think there is no way to live well while doing good; I think just the opposite. There is no way to do good without living well.

This book uses four central images to ground and inspire sustainable passion for social and personal transformation. Why images? Images help us to draw pictures of the life we want. Some people translate the verse from Genesis that says, "Let the waters bring forth swarms of living creatures," as "Let the waters draw pictures" (1:20). I use images and draw pictures as a way to train myself spiritually to be one who lives by the warmth of a simple sustainable fire.

The first image I want to use is that of the high-wire act: we learn to become "catchable" and "flyable," the words trapeze trainers use when a person is first allowed to fall into flying. Catchable is the experience of the grace that follows risk: we don't exactly fly so much as we give ourselves the permission to try to do so. We attempt what at first feels impossible. We fly as able-bodied flyers because we risk the possibility that we will be caught. "First we jump, then we get our wings." Ray Bradbury said something close to that when asked why he thought he could be a great writer. He had to try before he knew he could. Many of us stay on the far side of the high wire and just quiver because we don't have the courage to risk. To do good or to accomplish social transformation we must risk. We must move out of our comfort zone, try to walk the high wire, try to do what most people think can't be done. We fall into flying, and when we do so, we learn that we are catchable. Social change is not magical. It comes from the great combination of training and courage. We learn balance—and that balance allows us to walk the high wire between seemingly opposed matters, like living well and doing good.

We "fly through the air with the greatest of ease" when we get the right combination of living well and doing good. If all we do is "doing good," we would begin to look ridiculous, and with good reason; if all we do is "living well," we are living selfishly. Most of us want both: we want to do good in a way beyond caricature and self-righteousness; we want to live well in a way that is not selfish. The trapeze artist falls gracefully; the high-wire walker tries not to fall. Both are part of the image I imagine here.

The second image I want to propose is based in gathering wood and lighting fires. At one point I was becoming more deeply afraid about the energy crisis in America. I saw train wrecks everywhere I looked—whether it was the war in Iraq or the high prices of gasoline. At their heart these interacting disasters threatened my way of life as a middle-class American—as well as embarrassing my reputation as a successful social activist. The President told me to "drive less" and all I could do was laugh cynically—such individual solutions to systemic problems always amuse me. So one day I awoke a bit earlier in order to get on my bicycle and go collect twigs, a nature errand that is also a low-cost form of personal entertainment. I was particularly interested in apple wood, as it gives off a great smell. I would bike along, picking up good pieces of wood, filling up my bike basket. I realized I was ritualizing an act of hope. I was actually doing political liturgy—making pictures of the world I wanted. Did my activity resolve the energy crisis or stop the melting of the ice cap? I think not! But it did give me a way to touch the problem without getting burned.

I am sure I thought of this wood strategy because of a gift a friend had given in the midst of my despair. She was a neighbor in Miami. I had come from New England, and did not understand the woodlessness of the tropics. There was a beautiful fireplace in our house and I complained to her about not being able to find wood. Many mornings I would wake early to take my dog out, after she had taken hers out, only to find a pretty stack of four or five pieces of wood in my driveway, artfully assembled. Her picture moved me toward a measured simplicity.

These little trips were my way of "keeping a good light"—what they used to say about lighthouse-keepers. The third image for me is that of keeping a good light, of being a good lighthouse-keeper. Personal and social transformation are not firecrackers. They are not sporadic. They are long term. Lighthouse-keeping joins twig-gathering and high-wire walking to round out my imagistic method of living well and doing good. These images do give me a way to pray for a solution and to act one out in fairly silly ways. They give me my little fire to light at the end of my day. Most important of all, my ritual of twig-gathering transformed the source of my activism from sarcastic bitterness and despair to simple hope. I was able to imagine myself as a lighthouse-keeper and a high-wire walker, all through the simple act of gathering twigs.

While I do try to drive less, give money to organizations to fight for the environment against automobiles, attend endless meetings, read endless articles—while I activate my activism—I am also activating my spirit. Social change flows from "lit" spirits, not just from hard work. Working from simple images allows me to keep simple fires; it allows me to stay lit.

A fourth image rounds out my training in these images I use to become who I want to be. It is that of the firefly, which I see as the act of grace and the catalyst that keeps us going when we fall off the wire or lose our light. In June, our farm in Amherst is full of fireflies: the entire backyard lights up like a Christmas tree. The magic is even more beautiful to me because I remember watching my three children and the neighbor children chase the fireflies, night after night, and always fail to catch them.

The first three images all depend on something I have to do, but this last is all about being, not doing. We must sit still long enough to see the firefly fly by. My activist husband and I often say we wait for the next wave of social change. When it comes we want to surf it.

Our dilemma is simple enough: how do we live well while doing good? Do we save or savor the world? Which do we do today? Which tomorrow? I am not alone in this struggle. In his *New Yorker* story called "My Bird Problem," Jonathan Franzen describes it this way: "This was the scenario I had been at pains to avert for many years: not the world's falling apart in my future but in feeling inconveniently obliged to care about it in the present." Can you be well while doing good? Are simplicity and peace the opposites of activism and passion? Or are these sometimes opposites and sometimes friends? If so, how do we maximize the friendship and minimize the alienation? Is balance possible?

The balance comes from lighting simpler fires. It means doing small things well and fearing large things poorly done. It means fearing grandiosity above all. It means knowing what an enemy self-righteousness is to the activist, who must do less in order to achieve more.

An illustration: I once moved out of a house in Chicago because I couldn't stand the ugliness of the neighborhood anymore. I was deep in an activist period that required all my actions to be politically correct; I had to live in the right kind of neighborhood and think the right kind of thoughts and be with the right kind of people. I had taken my passion too far. My own personal morality had turned me into a self-righteous prig. I wanted to be right way too much. On the corner of our street was a bodega that every Monday morning put up a sign that said: "Five rolls of toilet paper for a dollar." It would stay up until Wednesday, when the owner would take it down. Every time I rounded the corner and went past his store to my house, I went berserk. Why could he not put beautiful fruits and vegetables out in front of his store? How dare he uglify the neighborhood in this way? I spoke to him often, making my absurd suggestions. Finally, I had to leave the neighborhood—he couldn't accept my suggestions and I couldn't accept his sign.

Instead, I could have used the Tai Chi approach to activism, to act without forcing, to move without requiring results. Tai Chi moves through air as though through water with calm. It is surely not passive, nor is it hyperactive. It is a flow, acting without forcing. Instead of my foolishness in Chicago, I could have made friends with the owner of the bodega. From time to time a basket of potatoes might have appeared in front of the store. Then again, it might not have.

Let me define some terms. By *simplicity* I mean a full day instead of a full week in one day. I mean a rich combination of action and reflection, merged daily in a pattern of living. I mean time alone, time in meetings, time with family, time to eat off real plates instead of from plastic containers.

By *peace* I mean being able to sleep at night. I mean deep confidence in who we are and what we are doing—with a simultaneous detachment from obvious short-term results. I mean a serious detachment from totalitarian attitudes toward social change by which we force our self-righteous will on the world: "We know what is good for you! That's why our lives are so miserable!" This message is too often both the surface and subliminal message of activism. Educator Paolo Freire declared it a disaster when the helper dominates the helped, but many activists engage that complexity daily.

By *activism* I mean acting to improve the world.

By *passion* I mean knowing that issues of justice and peace matter fundamentally, despite evidence to the contrary. There is no individual freedom from these matters. To imagine either that we are "self-made" or that "it is all up to us" is a fiction—the price of oil and global warming matter as much to our psyches and our social order as anything we do as individuals.

If simplicity is utter contentment, a contentment bordering on immorality in a world such as ours, passion is utter discontentment with the way things are. We have them both at the same time when we live as simple fires. We don't so much reduce our activist expectations as "right-size" them. We can't conquer the history of human selfishness personally. Getting our imagined victories and ourselves to a human size, a right size, joins humor in being a fine weapon against the peace of despair.

Another case in point: I was on my way to the anti-war demonstration held on September 25, 2005, taking the train from New York City to Washington, D.C. Amtrak had a switch failure at Newark and the train did not arrive. The other demonstrators waiting for the train got very mad: "The government has stopped the trains." "They did this on purpose." My fellow travelers began to demonstrate in circles around Penn Station, with loud, squeaky voices resembling nothing so much as the unwelcome voice of a flight attendant on a bad speaker telling us something we already know while we are trying to sleep. The rest of the passengers were also delayed; they also had risen early to get there. Here was an enormous opportunity to win anti-war friends. Instead, we went into a grumpy paranoia, which only drove us deeper inside our own despair—while turning off the other passengers. Why does the anti-war movement shoot

13

itself in the foot like this? Because it has failed to balance peace and passion.

It is very important for activists to be calm. The Gaelic word "calm" means to draw a circle around the soul, to protect it. That circle can both help and hurt us as we try to stay intensely alive and calmly happy. Learning to draw socially alert circles—to know when to open up to the stress of social change and when to close down—is the art of simplifiers. We light simple fires, not big ones. We keep them going through the night. We see ourselves as kindlers as much as burners.

As the first woman trained by Saul Alinsky and an almost gracefully aging hippie, as well as a mother, gardener, writer, and major goofballer, I have lived these questions for almost sixty years. I think I have a few answers, mostly learned from failures and restarts.

What do I know? Grace tells me to relax; justice pulls me to stressful caring. I live in between their push and pull, always knowing I am walking inner/outer home to the other "side." Grace keeps simplicity alive in me while a hunger for justice for others and myself often drives me.

Sacrifice, by the way, is not an answer to the question of balancing passion and simplicity. Activists do not have to sacrifice life well lived. Simplicity and passion are not opposites. A person can live passionately and quietly at the same time. We are both to save and savor the world; in fact, neither works without the other. Those who only savor collapse into an obnoxious, selfish hedonism; those who only save devolve into guilt-mongering bores. They yell at Amtrak workers in New York train stations at dawn because it is unthinkable to them that they are not in control of the world.

I call the simplifying strategy "simple fires" because the paradox is important. Most people who claim they are "burned-out" have really never been lit; they smolder rather than burn. Simplifiers "do what we can, where we are, with what we have." Some of us do it hopefully, and others do it without hope. Simplifiers are also very careful about the words "success" and "failure." We don't expect to completely transform the world. In the Hebrew Bible, according to Abraham Joshua Herschel's interpretation, we are neither to save the world nor to be free from caring about saving the world. We are to be very careful not to be grandiose in our passionate care for the neglected and oppressed—including the parts of ourselves who are neglected or oppressed. We keep our vision well lit—and we also relax and play with the dog. How dare we play with the dog when people are suffering? We dare in the name of the very life that we are protecting.

We act for good while living well because we are—as Gandhi put it—the work we seek. If activists cannot demonstrate in their own lives the abundant justice they demand of the world, then there is no point in speaking because they will not be heard. Witness is the method that the activist uses to best effect, not telling others what to do, finger-wagging, guilt-tripping, or "sacrificing" for the cause. We are driven not by outer success but inner desire to make the world a better place. We act but we do not force. The desire to conquer is itself a form of subjection. We end up mimicking the behavior of the people whose ways we are trying to change.

Simplicity is the privilege of privileging the inner world. It is the art of sustainable choice. It is turning up the volume on some messages and turning it down on others. Simplifiers light and sustain simple fires. We see the beauty of a pile of small sticks in our driveway. Light and warmth and balance result.

 CHAPTER TWO

SIMPLIFYING MONEY

W hy start with money? Money complicates more things than anything else. We believe we need it and do many things that are not our own in order to get it. Many of our jobs are about money, not vocation. Much of our time is spent to secure ourselves even though our cupboards are groaning full. What we really need from money is a strategy, a way of thinking about it.

Once in South Africa, a limping boy, perhaps age six, approached me. He wanted a nickel. I gave it to him, only to be overwhelmed by fifty other children within minutes. To give each of them a nickel only meant the multiplication of misery and sorrow surrounding me in a Capetown Street. I also knew that I didn't have a nickel for all the children. Nor did I have compassion to match the crowd. I was no longer feeling compassionate about that boy; I had become afraid. I was scared stiff of the raw human need that surrounded me.

On that day, once I recovered from my fear of the children, I vowed to come up with principles on which to base the original compassion and generosity that I felt toward that child. My giving would no longer be spur of the moment. Indeed, now I say no to all beggars on behalf of long-term sustainable change against poverty. I do not give out even spare change. Nor did I give to the victims of Hurricane Katrina: so many others did that I felt I needed to stick to my long-term principle of transformational, sustainable change in the human condition. Have I become hard of heart? Or sharp of mind? Or both? No. I have become a right-sized human being who wants to both live well and do good. I want to do my part. I am even willing to do more than my part. I am not willing to spend my one precious life in guilt. Guilt insults God, that South African boy, and me. He does not need my guilt. He needs my money, well spent to create a good world for him and all his friends. He needs my money; what I need is principles to guide me.

How are we to decide how to be effectively charitable? Especially as we age and enjoy the benefits of the money we have earned, these demands can become excruciating. Charitable giving deserves the same kind of planning we use for retirement or for a trip. It deserves thought, followed by action.

When I say strategy about money, what I really mean is a set of principles. Money complicates our lives precisely because we don't know what we really think about it. Nothing is so emblematic as our deceit when we say, "It's not about the money." Indeed it often *is* about the money! But we don't know how to say what we mean by that. I believe we live well and do good when we value money but not overmuch. We don't need to apologize for our interest in money, nor do we need to become its slave.

What follows are the six principles that ground my own strategy about money. There is nothing new about these principles that guide me. They come from my desire to keep a good light and to light simple fires. They come from the awe and grace I feel when I see fireflies light up the night. They are ways to navigate the high wire of lofty demands and minute capacity: the folk saying for that is "the ocean is so big and my boat is so small." While there is nothing new about these principles, they do need to be newly understood because the world is even bigger than it was when they were first thought up.

1. The widow's mite

You will recall that in the biblical story of the widow and her mite, when the widow makes her offering in the Temple Jesus praises her small gift over the large gifts that wealthier people give. He particularly praises her humility over their self-aggrandizement. This is what the Japanese call *kazen*, the importance of small things. I know I can't do enough. I can do hardly anything at all. I begin with an appreciation of my size.

2. Compassionate generosity

We need to feel a compassionate generosity beyond writing a check. I give out of joy that I can give, out of joy in the world that has come into being for Capetown children. "My body blazed that I was blessed and could bless" is how one poet puts it. We are stewards of God's abundance and joyful heralds of the banquet, which means that when we do give, we give from a sense of feast, not famine—the way God gives to us. Sometimes I want to replace the word "steward-ship" with the word "praise." Bill Green of the United Church of Christ says stewardship is about doxology first and foremost. Giving from an overflowing fountain is God-like; giving from guilt and grief—to just make the starving children go away—is selfish at its root. That refusal to change ourselves into joy before we give hurts the world more than anything else we could do.

3. Dependency versus responsibility

Less spiritual but more politically acceptable is the principle of refusing to create dependency. That boy in Capetown is not my fault or my problem. However, he is my responsibility. The civil rights leader Malcolm X said of racism, "It is not my fault but it is my responsibility." When we think racism and poverty are our fault, we create dependency, especially if we are successful in fighting them.

Paolo Freire, the South American educational theorist, said that when we give we have to make sure we don't harm the ones to whom we give. That means paying attention to our own souls as much as to those of others. It also means paying attention to power dynamics. I will never forget a woman I encountered on a bus in China. We were traveling together with a large group. At every stop she got off the bus and encouraged the hoards of children to come to her. She then asked someone to photograph her as she gave out "nickels."

4. Giving our best

When I give, I want it to be my best. When I go to the potluck of principles about money, I want one of my dishes to be the best on the table. I want an excellent principle and a principal of excellence to guide me. Why? Because of pride, because of fun, because I can. These may not be the height of morality, but they are a way of getting at the issue of money. I want to teach myself joy in giving it away. My gift may be small but that doesn't mean it can't have quality. I want the best cheese in my macaroni dish, the best green chilies. I want to be remembered as a high-ranking member of the society of the gift exchange.

I remember a local food bank filling up with cranberry sauce, right after a cranberry food-scare hit the news. People were giving away their worst and not their best. I want to give gourmet food to the poor and to hope for a world where everyone eats as well as I do today.

5. Power to change

I want my gifts to have power, and I don't mean coercive power. Instead, I want to change human conditions. I want to stop poverty, not merely ameliorate it. Often charity replaces the search for justice. Sometimes it is better to take political acts against poverty than to give to relief efforts. Often we hear not a peep from the populace about poverty. Some generosity involves peeping loud and long.

When I say power, I mean the kind that is demonstrated in the art of Tai Chi: we act without forcing. We don't insist on our way, even if our way is good. We act, politically and spiritually. We don't force our agenda on the world, but we do want to move and change things. Our compassion for Capetown boys is not about guilt. Nor is it about greed, an unusually strong sin in many activists. We think that by "doing good" we can make ourselves look much better. We can salve our ego by feeding children. The power we want is bound neither by grace nor greed: instead, it is a deep urgency to transform the world so that some don't have what others cannot have.

Most of our charity comes from our softer side. It is often impulsive. A wiser approach insists on actually doing something for someone. A wiser approach is more often hard-nosed and systemic. I also tithe my income (after taxes) to organizations that do justice. I did not give to Katrina victims. I did not give during 9/11. I was too deeply aware that the Red Cross would have to give away unused blood because the administrative structure to deliver the blood would simply not exist. I also skipped the tsunami, even though my entire denomination (the UCC) gave its money there instead of to a long-term campaign to increase membership in our congregations. I gave to the campaign (the Still Speaking Initiative) because I want to build fire trucks and enlarge the base for long-term charitable work, not put out fires.

I choose a few organizations and give them larger gifts. Why? So I can have a say in their work and keep an eye on what is going on in the board, the staff, and therefore the actual work. Rather than being allergic to administrative infrastructure, I pay for it. I want it to be brilliant. In the same way that good investors invest in stocks by reviewing the business plan and executive leadership of a corporation, I want my charitable dollar to be well delivered to social change that eliminates begging in the first place. I have no illusions that this is simple. In fact, I believe that people who are crazy enough to give their lives to such a project should be paid a lot, have great staff, great stationery, great administrative capacity. I find the "anti-administration" notion of many charitable givers to be naive. It results in embarrassing things like boxes of unused and unusable clothing flooding New Orleans—or worse, blood poured down the drain.

6. The empty offering plate
When it comes to money and living well and doing good—all three in one sentence—we understand the image of the empty offering plate. It is empty precisely in order to be filled. We know that it is important to empty in order to be filled. When we give we find ourselves involved in the paradox of giving to get, of emptying to fill. Had I not been so full of myself that day in South Africa, I might have made a wiser set of decisions.

We live extravagantly amid scarcity. We are managers of extravagance. We enter the emptiness to be filled. Then we are able to give, once our spirits are filled. We give from a great sense of paradox. We too are in need. We too need to be filled. Giving away what we have fills us. We understand the central gospel paradox that we can have only what we are able to let go of.

Practically speaking, these principles can be fulfilled in two ways. One is the Christian practice of tithing, in which we take ten percent of our income (after taxes) and give it to a congregation, charity, or the poor. Why after taxes? Because generous people like paying taxes. We think government may be able to do more than we ever can. We want systemic justice, not charity. I often recommend giving five percent to our own congregations and assuring ourselves that it is the kind of place involved in systemic change. The other five percent goes to organizations that change things or to political movements, or to the organizations whose envelopes flood our mailboxes—our colleges, fraternities, schools, and the like.

The other way to fulfill these principles is to follow the Jewish law of *Tzedekah*, which is a many-tiered understanding of giving, with nine practical principles. The first principle is to assure your own security so as not to be a burden to others; indeed securing yourself is understood as a virtue. Second, you secure those of blood relation, again so as not to make your family a burden on the larger community. Third, you give to people and organizations you know, in an ascending order of anonymity, with the final and highest level of virtue being to give to those you do not know, cannot know and who will never know you. This practice—which has a thousand versions and more adherents—results in an astonishing number of anonymous gifts given to symphonies, operas, and the like. Unknown people benefit from the gifts of people they can never thank. This hierarchy of giving is extraordinarily useful to the person who feels a compassionate generosity and wants to make a difference.

In neither approach are we required to give all. Instead, we are to discipline the portion that is spare change. Once a theological position is taken and a strategy developed, we are free to walk the streets and open the envelopes. We can say both yes and no, with vigor. Not only do we enjoy a deeper peace of mind, but real people really benefit, which is the point in the first place. What we can spare spares others. What we can earn helps others. Why are some people allergic to earning money? Because we are lacking in principals that guide us in how to spend it.

To speak of the switch we make from unconscious to conscious giving, or fear and trembling to principle-guided giving, we can use just one phrase: *We move from famine* (of thought) *to feast* (of thought).

The biblical story about the wedding feast is a great story to show this shift. Jesus turns the water into wine. As well as a story about a wedding feast, it is a warning away from famine into feast, away from scarcity into plenty. It is also a story about the endtime: even better things are coming than have come before. For those of us who live in times of spiritual famine (most notably expressed in the epidemic "time famine" of first-world people) and those of us who live in times of doom (as in, when will the next bad thing happen and how?), this story is a glorious antidote. It says two things on two levels: one is that feast will (miraculously) beat out famine as metaphor and actuality for life. It also says that things at the end will be better than they were at the beginning. The good wine is saved until last. When we give in principled ways we do so on behalf of hope in the future.

Let me define what I mean by *famine*. Famine is the reigning myth. It is king and queen, emperor and president.

As the kids would say, "It rules." Myth one is that *there is not enough*. You will barely get through an hour anywhere in the first-world without the subtext of "there is not enough" coming up. "I would love to come but I am so busy."

Myth two is that *more is better*. "When I get the promotion or the gig or the partner, then I will have the more I need to be better."

Myth three is that *there is nothing you can do about it*. "I won't get the promotion or the gig or the partner, and if I do it won't work out, so there is really nothing to do but stay here and whine about it along with the rest of the culture."

Myth four—and this is really a new one, straight from the Republicans—is that *you are personally responsible*. No pension? You must have invested your 401K wrong. No health insurance? You probably didn't take good care of your health. No freedom from work? You probably went to the wrong graduate school.

These four myths are relatives. They all belong to the same family. They dine very well together every night. There is not enough. More is better. There is nothing you can do about it. You are personally responsible.

Once I started to get to know this family of ruling myths, I found them everywhere. They are like a Rorschach or one of those kids' art games. You know, find the donkey in the picture, and once you do you can't quite see anything else.

The story of the wedding at Cana is a striking alternative to the king, queen, prince, and princess myths. It says just the opposite: there is plenty, we have enough, there are lots of things you can do to change things, and we are positively personally responsible. There is not blame here—as in who ordered the wrong amount of wine—but there is hope. As they will say at the World Social Forum, over and over again, another world is possible.

I am a recovering famine freak. I am training myself to be a feast freak. I choose small strategic gifts. I choose a feast mentality (even though there are plenty of days of desperation and despair still left). I also choose a steady principled pace that has plenty of time for setbacks—as well as plenty of time built into it for my money to create lasting change. Boys in South Africa will be less desperate some day. The better wine is coming. That is the first and central point of view I have on money. From there the rest is simpler.

 CHAPTER THREE

SIMPLIFYING CONTROL

Those of us who believe in the possibility of good—"simplifiers"—sustain our belief by letting impossibility have its way with us. We are like good parents in that we choose our battles with our teenagers. We don't make them pick up their room every day. We let some things go. Oddly, the more we let go, the more we can often achieve.

There is a balance to understanding time and human potential. We will not live long enough to change all that needs changing or all that annoys us or all that diminishes us, but we will be able to balance our objectives and our actions into some meaningful personal agenda. That will require the art of saying "no" as well as saying "yes." The Leave It Alone committee decides the pitches that we "take" in baseball's wonderful word. Sometimes we shake our head "no" to the catcher. We just don't want to pitch the pitch; we know the batter can hit, we know it's not ours, we know it's just not right. Sometimes we nod our head "yes" to the catcher: we want to throw that pitch. We think it will be a good pitch at this time in this game. We do everything on a choice-by-choice basis.

Making decisions about whether to be active or passive is part of the art of simplification. Both have value. Sometimes we build small fires and sometimes we just leave some sticks on the ground for another day. I believe that most activists would be twice as good if they worked half as hard. That is the math of living well while doing good.

Many over-busy people take whatever is thrown at them and think they have to respond to it all. These are the people who open all their mail, return all their phone calls, and have early heart attacks. People who simplify control make choices. We have a "yes" capacity as well as a "no" capacity. We work for the fires that will get lit and stay lit. That is how we deserve the accolade that we "kept a good light." The Leave It Alone committee has as large an agenda as the Let's Do It committee.

Does this mean we are passive? No way. We are active in the best sense of the word: we *choose* our actions. We choose actions that we can actually control and follow through on. We do not choose everything because we know we can't follow through on everything—and we even like the words "follow through." If I could have found the wisdom, time, and sense to follow through on more of my activist and organizational projects, I would have improved the world. Instead, I often created a history of raised and dashed expectations. I harmed what I intended to help in the spirit of activism. "Follow through" is not a dirty word; like "administration," it is a beautiful word and deed. I remember a joke someone made about me once. It's not the kind I forget: "She did not chew everything she bit off." Yes, many of us bite off more than we can chew.

When it comes to following through—the ability to send thank-you notes after the event, to sit with a cup of tea and enjoy the warmth of the messed-up room, to have enough lead time for the evaluation so that people can really think about what happened—it is important to remember that every good action requires three times as much time as we think it will. There is the long beginning, the action, then the follow-up. When we give up control, we do so in the name of wanting to do things beautifully and right. We act like the black preacher who said, "I am an African preacher, and I take my time." We learn to control our time by subtracting how much we will do of "everything."

The concept of *whole-cost accounting* made popular by Hazel Henderson, a Canadian economist, is a helpful tool as we seek to give up control. By that phrase she means that we charge the full cost of our supposed "bargains" to our own accounts, not just the amount we handed over. We may pay $100 for a tree and have it delivered for $25. The earth also pays a price, but that price is rarely noticed. When we find bargains at Wal-Mart we should also account for the unjust labor practices and lack of medical coverage that are part of the package—when people without insurance get sick, they end up on our tax bills. Likewise, the cost of a tank of gas is not just the price per gallon, but the damage to the environment and the theft of picnics from our grandchildren, who may or may not be able to go outside. People who do whole-cost accounting do so as a way to honor the environment— the air and water we require for living. When we dishonor the air and water, bad things happen to our children, to other people's children, and to us, not to mention what happens to animals. Whole-cost accounting takes a hard look at "bargains" and wonders if there really is such a thing.

In whole-cost accounting we also remember the voices of the natural world, so many of which have already disappeared. Many scientists argue that one-third of all birdcalls are already gone. They are part of our gasoline pump "bargains" and the chemicals we spray on our lawns to make them look green. In the process of living lives that are too full and too phony—like the color of grass fertilized chemically—we have already lost so many important things. We need not lose any more; ironically, though, we will only save what is about to be lost by letting go of some of the things we think we must have.

When we account for the whole cost of a driving or eating experience, we remember what is gone and we celebrate what still is—and we find a place in our heart for the melting ice of the Poles, for the forgotten frog, for the great matrix of being that keeps our home in New York City connected to your home in Montana. We listen to voices that are too often silenced. We both experience a shiver of grace and declare an emergency. We want nature to have a strong voice in the great choir of our lives. We even want to pay for its many blessings to us. We do not want farmers to sell low; we want farmers to sell high and we want to pay higher prices for our produce. We want it to be wholesome: what good is it if the food we got for a bargain gives us cancer?

When we do whole-cost accounting, we give sound to the silence. We let nature and justice have their voice at our gas pump and at our table. We rise from the death of the false bargain into the life of the true cost of living.

There is a link, in my view, between the words "terra" and "terror." The link is that until nature's balance has sound and speech, we will continue to silence it. That silence will destroy us. *Terra firma*, earth foundational, is something that must be shared with all. Otherwise there are no bargains left, whatsoever, for anyone. People who live well and do good also know real *terror*: we know what has been lost and how we could lose even more. We manage our time and our life with deft attention to activity and passivity. We are even prepared to pay for it by using Community Supported Agriculture or Farm Shares or Farmer's Markets whose produce seems more expensive at first glance but actually are less expensive when we do whole-cost accounting.

We buy less and emphasize quality once we see whole-cost accounting as a way of being. We say "no" to more so we can say "yes" to a few things and say it well. We give up fantasies of being big and grand on behalf of being small and beautiful. We control our desires. We remember that authority is nothing more or less than the ability to control oneself.

Whole-cost accounting is also a time-management concept. We actively try to control what we can, while knowing that every single activity has a multiplicity of dimensions to it. We let some things go so that we can actually focus on the wholeness of each action. We have both a Let's Do It committee and a Leave It Alone committee—and we know when to work with each one.

How dare we think of ourselves as large or powerful in a world where even the Hubble telescope can't see all the stars? How dare we try to improve on the world God has made? More importantly, improve the world in the name of what? In the name of savoring or saving? In the name of controlling or freeing? In the name of an idolatrous "we who know better"? Or in the name of creation itself, which God has been trying to restore to perfection for a long time? Are activists trying to control or improve the world? This is not a small question. Knowing the answer for oneself as an activist is key to all the rest of the effort.

Simplifiers restore creation as quiet junior partners with God. What little we do is done with the hope that it contributes to the restoration of the original blessing of creation. The praise all goes to God, who is great precisely because of this bothering with the specks of DNA that we are.

A large dose of self-importance is not warranted, but a small one appears to be legitimate. We may dare to imagine

LIVING WELL WHILE DOING GOOD

ourselves as grand (and as unpretentious) as a good light-house-keeper who, on behalf of the Almighty, keeps a good light. Simplicity is the right size dress on the right size woman. It understands how small and yet significant we are. Simplicity gets us to the right size—the right size for our days and the right size for our hope. Getting this inner edge on our outer expectations is the trick to understanding the matter of control. We do act but we do not control. It is not that taking care of the earth and its peoples is not important to us; it is just an inch less important than the inner world, which tells us we are not God, first and foremost. In the name of this inner life, I gather twigs. I know such a gathering is ridiculous. I also know it is beautiful.

Most of us live under the commandment to get bigger and better. Most of us are sitting in an economy-class seat while always looking for an upgrade. We want to have the better seat, the better view, and the better opportunities. While activists spend a lot of time condemning this kind of materialism and consumerism, we are often complicit. The more people who come to our meetings, the better we are doing. The more people who give money to our organization, the more successful we are. We obey the commandments of our culture while trying to change it—but "the master's tools will not fell the master's house," writes Audre Lord, quite poignantly. She is right. We need to get our expectations right. "Too much" topples us. "Too little" embarrasses us. When I argue that activists need to name their own measures of success—how many calls, how many meetings, how many hours—I do so in the name of balance and sustainability.

When we get the size of our expectations right, we do simple things well. This morning I took my new dog on a walk. He came to us from Miami and had never felt cold, never seen snow, never seen stairs. He resisted each new experience the first time—sitting at the bottom of the stairs and refusing to climb, feeling the snow on his feet and trying to jump up in the air, looking dumfounded when he climbed out of the airplane carrier in Connecticut after leaving the tropics only three hours earlier. What impressed me was that he was only afraid *once*. After he managed each cold and fear, he went on and didn't repeat the fears over and over. He is another companion on the road to simplicity, where we don't have time for repeated fears of the cold.

There is a characteristically modern kind of evil: indirect, impersonal, and mediated by complex organizations and institutional roles. We can't even touch its stairs, let alone climb them. So systemic and invisible are the forces that bind us, and especially bind the poor, that some of us get depressed when we can't find that first stairstep every day. Our minds are as colonized as countries once were: we internalize the very capitalism we criticize, and then we lie to ourselves about how we have done no such thing. It is no wonder that the social order has such staying power, if the very doing of our good gets in the way of our living well. We need to get to our right size, know that many things are way beyond us, and still find the first step on the stairs, take it, and learn how to tame our fear.

I was warned this morning by deer tracks in the snow outside my door. They warned me of enchantment, of the animal spirit. They warned me of the arrogance and far-fetched dangerous fantasy of "thinking locally and acting globally." What could any of it mean compared to deer tracks in the snow or remembering to sweep off that dark front porch which, once iced up, stays iced all winter? So much of our lives ice up all winter. So much of fear refuses to be tamed by the animal within us. Animals don't have the fantasy of being gods. They are free from that in a way that humans are not.

Humor is another good tool for simplifiers, the finest tool that the Leave It Alone committee has. I remember being invited by the Junior League of Miami to give an "inspirational" speech at their annual banquet. I asked what their current programs were. "Domestic violence, incest, rape, reproductive rights," they responded. Then immediately my contact, the president, continued, "We'd like something light, upbeat, hopeful." I dare say I had a good inner laugh. Who does she think I am?

When I was invited to give a pro-choice speech to three hundred college students and activists, I went straight to my daughter. What could I possibly say?, I asked her. Did they want me to drop the whole weight of forty years on this issue, with the right to choose still not secured? She responded with a singular beauty: "Mom, what you don't understand is that kids my age just want to belong. Tell them they belong to a historical movement for women's rights. Tell them they belong to a great cause. Then sit down." I followed her advice. I acted as a simple fire instead of a bonfire. I kept a good light. I didn't fall off my high wire with hopes that were impossibly heavy to carry.

We play our role and then we rest. Humor and perspective help us make the decision about which role to wear, which pitch to take—and humor knows especially that we can't have too many costumes in our closet.

The Leave It Alone committee also knows when to turn off the engine. Late one afternoon we went for a sail at dusk on

Biscayne Bay. We were out for about four hours when our captain turned toward home. Usually in other sails she had turned on the engine as we approached the dock. Her boat— a sailing instructor's boat—is docked at the far end of the marina in a corner, a bit of a tight squeeze but not impossible with the engine going. This night she got a twinkle in her eye as we turned toward home. "Let's try it without the engine. I think the conditions are right." Minutes later she added, "We may have to turn the engine on at the last minute, so be ready. We won't know until we get close." Moments later we glided, soundlessly and effortlessly, into the berth.

The calm in that moment deserves respect and attention. It was more "quiet" than I have ever heard. I used to think you couldn't hear quiet, but now I know you can. It also took less effort than I have experienced in a long time. Effort is a persistent intruder in my life: even getting to this afternoon of sailing had required it. Did I have time? Would it be enough fun to justify the time off? Did I bring the right dish for my part of the potluck? Being engineless, however, was an utterly new experience.

Enginelessness is on the other side of effortlessness: it is not the absence of struggle so much as the presence of peace. I want more life with the engine off. I want its quiet most of all. The clamor for justice is so large in my head that I can't take its clamor all the time, nor do I think many people can. The result of nonstop noise and the effort that creates it causes us to forget the root of our desire in the deepest of peace. In his essay "Small Silences: Listening for the Lessons of Nature," the nature writer and lion-tamer Edward Hoagland writes, "It is hard to even find a sight line without buildings, pavement, people . . . and we're not even awed by each other any more. Even people are too much of a good thing." As a biologist, Hoagland thinks that God created the world for the bubbles, the froth. In other words, God was not worried about getting from one place to the other, but developed engines for their fun and froth, their evidence of the magnificence of creation. "Glee is like the froth on a beer or on cocoa," Hoagland writes. "Not essential. Glee is effervescence. It is bubbles in the water, beyond efficiency, which your thirst doesn't actually need."

Turning off the engine is a good idea if we want peace or beauty or quiet in our life. You don't have to be a poet to understand this meaning, just an ordinary person living an ordinary life. Interior decorators know this, and "Fewer Finer" is what every decorator will tell you. They hate clutter and love open space. Gardeners do too. Pruning a bush makes it grow beautifully. Letting it overtake your yard does not. Activists who do something for justice rather than everything for justice understand that less is frequently more.

What do we do if we agree that there is more to abundance than "more"? What if we are ashamed of just how much we want to control? What if we are ready to live at our right size? But what if at the same time we don't know how to say "no" to a starving child or put up with political corruption?

We can appoint a Leave It Alone committee. If you haven't appointed one yet for the home and for the office, I invite you to do so. Many wise people say that experience is something you don't get until just after you need it. Most of us know that grace is God's unconditional acceptance—but we rarely apply this notion practically. Instead we live by our to-do lists, our accomplishments, and numbers and assessments not our own. Most of us live in the "time famine" and "culture of haste" so completely that we are in danger of permanently cluttering our spiritual and physical space because we don't have enough time. We are like the

Red Sox in certain ways, whose score always seems to be Destiny 7, Red Sox 6.

How do we get out of this perpetual cycle of defeat? First of all, we do not, like Pilate, wash our hands of the matter. That is the worse thing we can do. We can instead commit civil disobedience of sacralizing time and keeping Sabbath. We can say "no" to culture and "yes" to grace. We can refer lots of things to the Leave It Alone committee. We can then choose what fits into our size 8 or 14 dress: we can focus and do one or two things, maximum three, very well.

Specifically, we can become carefully measured in our own personal job descriptions. I make ten important phone calls a week, and answer what comes in if I have time afterward. The Leave It Alone committee handles the calls I don't get to. It does about as good a job as I would do if I got to the people beyond my capacity to reach in a human way. My agenda is to be sure my parish is well taken care of and that I notice, remember, and touch those who are in need and those who are well. That little measurement has saved me from being at the beck and call of others. I have other measurements built into my job description because I am so aware how many other people would like to run my life and job for me. I prefer to do it myself.

Every day the calendar can threaten to take us over or we can use it to create margins and breathing spaces in our life. I keep at least ten moments open in my calendar every day. These moments are rituals, or habits—they may take less than a minute or at least an hour. They are my touchstones: to write a little, to walk a little, to garden a little, and to do one domestic job in my house that doesn't have to be done (like the dishes). I work the corners and do a little bit every day—and thus am able to keep a relatively orderly home and garden, as well as write a book from time to time and attend in ritual ways to the needs of my body for health. As I age I actually grade myself on whether I do the aerobic, stretching, and weight-lifting parts of my workout or not. Yes, I am a workaholic in need of many disciplines to have a life, and my work is actually the enemy of my personal health.

These are the top four priorities for the life that is called mine and they each need an hour a day. I like to book them in first. Usually the domestic "moment" gets reduced to cleaning out the sock drawer—but the rest often find their way into real time. The rest of the day I work for others. In these touchstones, I live for myself. I also "touch" with consciousness my partner, Warren, my three kids, my work, and my communications. These are the middle four of the ten. To be me, I "work" family and job. I am conscious of the need to do this every day, even on holidays.

Finally, there are two more things I like to do every day and it is embarrassing that these are often the most hurried and flurried. These are luxuries, and the first is to do something funny or dramatic or strange or outside the boxes of my life. I call this ninth touchstone "drama." The tenth is to do something for the poor or neglected, even if it is nothing more than praying for them.

This list of ten touchstones is my measurement for my life. They are my rituals. It is a good day if I touch all ten points and a decent day if I get to eight. If something comes along that doesn't fit into these ten, I refer it to the Leave It Alone committee.

Additionally, I maintain a personal mission statement when these smaller guides get fuzzy and I either don't know what to do or do more than I should or can. The personal mission statement is: *I am made for Spiritual Nurture and for Public Capacity.* Both, not either. If I am spending too much time holding people's hands, it is time for my ministry to push them toward an adventure. If I have been pushing people too hard toward social change or adventure or both, it is time for me to hold some hands and provide some consolation and comfort. I try to hold this tension together in myself and in others.

Finally, if I get too tight about these measurements or missions, I emphasize the drama part of the basic "tens." I either hope something wonderful will happen or I make it happen. Which means that serendipity—the finding of something on your way to finding something else—is queen of the day.

We rarely admit the fact that most of our days and most of our lives are unfinished symphonies. I prefer to admit that through my large number of referrals to the Leave It Alone committee—and then I aggressively try to finish and refinish the life I was meant to live. I want to live well and do good so much that I am willing to not do so on behalf of doing so. I want to hold together the seeming paradox of virtue and pleasure—and that takes measured activity and measured inactivity—both, not either. Both simplicity and fire result, and that is the point of living well and doing good. We pitch and the universe bats. We make our pitches as good as they can get. Then we let go.

 CHAPTER FOUR

SIMPLIFYING CONFLICT

Conflict is everywhere—at family dinner tables, family reunions, the United Nations, and in most countries. No virtuous person will be far from conflict for long. In our urge to make a difference in the world, we will run smack dab straight on into human pessimism, cynicism, and grief over failed attempts at goodness. The majority of people will not want a good person to succeed at anything. They won't know why: they will simply know how important it is for them to sneer at decent objectives.

People who want to live well while doing good can anticipate a life in which conflict is normal, inevitable, ordinary, expected. The cultural messages tell us we must choose between our own pleasure or the world's service, our own time or time dedicated to others. It's either "You have to take care of Number One" or "Life is relationships and taking care of others." There are countless versions of these two diametrically opposed life views, and many people just fall off the high wire, drop to the ground, and sit there in a muddle. Those who want to walk the wire and not fall will have to face early and often the reality that conflict will be present in every single setting. For breakfast, should they go to the park and sit alone with a high-priced coffee, or should they sit with the child or husband who has become dull or demanding? Or should they attend a breakfast meeting, the real bane of existence for most activists and high-flying professionals? Conflicts like how to have breakfast are normal but only the beginning. Added to them are conflicts about whether to go to the gym or answer more email, take a walk after dinner or return a few phone calls, enjoy lunch at the river or read a professional article at our desk, with the Styrofoam take-out not far away.

Those who want to live well and do good, however, will befriend conflict. We will make it our own. We will become experts at it. We will enjoy it. We will predict it, anticipate it, tame it, laugh at it, and revel in it. "Of course," we will say, "there are always two-plus choices for every moment." I am a choice-maker. I make choices. I choose X sometimes and Y other times and I suffer the loss of the one I don't choose. I am not afraid to suffer. I sometimes choose X and Y at the same time. But I only choose a small pile of X twigs and a small pile of Y twigs. I go slowly. I am rarely the captive of what I don't have and more the captive of what I do have.

I sometimes call this conflict-loving, choice-making capacity that of the *tough dove*. There is nothing soft about making choices all the time and there is actually something very hard about it. We turn down people who want us. We really say "no." We get negative feedback. The people to whom we say "no" will not like it. The people to whom we say "yes" will rarely reward us, either. Tough doves live beyond both praise and criticism in an inner world they have created for themselves. They are highly strategic, highly directed, highly focused at any given moment. Tough doves make tough choices.

Simultaneously, tough doves get buried under and snowed over. They also lose their way in the snow and fog of human interaction. They can feel like they are constantly digging out from a snowstorm. The desk that looked clear on Monday can be buried by Wednesday. I often feel that my own life is a constant climbing out of a desk stress hole. The people to whom I should write, the people whom I should thank join the people at whom I should yell and the endless letters I should, as a democratic citizen, be sending to my representatives. They all combine to turn me into something as small and inconsequential as a dove. We go from tough to dove and back again in minutes.

The first way to survive the omnipresence of conflict is to expect it and to develop an internal mantra: "Here comes my old friend, Conflict. She has been here before." When I hear conflict knocking on my door or in my belly, I often hum an old hymn, "Drop thy still dews of quietness, till all our conflicts cease." When it comes to conflict, we can have tragic results or comic results. By my spiritual training (singing my hymn), by my waiting and my befriending of conflict, I am able to at least hope for comic endings to conflicts. Tough doves work for the comedy, the happy ending. Tough people work to win; winning ends in tragedy.

Just recently I had to hire a person whose references were not strong, but I liked her in my own gut and my own way. She was an African-American woman who had raised questions about anti-gay behavior in a previous internship. Needless to say, she was punished for raising a question that the senior pastor had not addressed. He was on one page on the issue and she on the other, so her very simple act of raising the subject was seen as "making trouble." The fact that it was not her fault mattered not at all. She was still considered a troublemaker, and other people on my hiring committee had heard the same thing. Plus, there was another rumor cooking: when she got in trouble in a white context, she "played the race card." Whatever that means! These very short coded statements go a long way toward making people conflict-averse. Getting to the bottom of what they mean is what tough doves do: we expect conflict, we like conflict; we think conflict is the way through relationships. I hired the person. I have been richly rewarded by her trouble-making. Why? Because I can't imagine how we get through these kinds of issues without trouble. If she were, however, to accuse me, a white woman, of racism, you can bet I would be hurt. So why would I not welcome her trouble into my system? Just to avoid getting hurt? I don't think so.

In addition to training ourselves for tough dove conversations, we also learn the art of meetings. Meetings are sometimes the most toxic and hurtful place in the world. I just read an agenda from an old meeting in my new church. The first statement on the list was, "Refrain from saying mean things that have already been said or increasing the hurt that exists." I wasn't at that meeting—but I have been at that meeting!

Simplifiers practice the art of meeting and the art of conversation. We become tough in our dovelike behavior. We sustain it. We become known for it. After all, any human encounter is a meeting. A dinner party, a baseball game, a doctor's appointment—these are all meetings. Tough doves learn to love meetings and to turn them into an art form. We begin by anticipating that there will be conflict in every meeting, and that some of it may even be hurtful. We may find ourselves in a conflict with the doctor's receptionist over the insurance form or with people behind us who are cursing at our slowness or with colleagues at dinner when someone simply sucks all of the air out of the room. How do we get through the little conflicts—and the big ones that follow them? We learn to love conflict. We hum. We give our innocence to the Leave It Alone committee and put a big smile on our face when conflict arises. She is our friend; we know about her. We know how to listen. We know how to ask questions. "Donna, I think you are a racist." "Tell me more." The words "tell me more" are the very best response we can give to any charge against us. When we immediately say, "No, I am not," it only fuels the fire.

If William Sloane Coffin was right in saying that "the world is too dangerous for anything but truth and too small for anything but love," we who open our mouths on a daily basis have a lot to learn. We need to practice how we speak and how we listen. "Tell me more" is a great response to the arrival of conflict. And then we need to shut up and to truly listen.

Many people argue that every conflict and every complaint is simply an unmet need. Somebody needs something they aren't getting. Why wouldn't we want them to get what they want? Why would we want to be stuck in that all-too-human *cul de sac* of "It's not my fault" and "You're wrong"? Why would we not listen?

Once we understand that conflict is inevitable, we find ourselves in need of concrete strategies to resolve it. How we use our tongues, how we use our mouths, how we use our speech is the best strategic first step. It is not an accident that parents intervene in children's squabbles to say, "Use your words, not your fists." Neither is it an accident that parents find themselves saying, "Watch your mouth." Using our words well can contribute to peace in the kitchen and peace in the world. Practicing the words "Tell me more" goes a long way toward resolving conflict. Very often if our antagonist is truly heard, we may become free also to truly speak.

Often we can avoid ridiculous conflicts by creating an environment of appreciation around us. Living well involves finding our tongue's way to praise. We learn to be appreciative in a world of severe appreciation deficits. Simply: find something to appreciate even in a situation or person you adamantly dislike. Become known for speaking this way. Such speech can and does change the world, and it doesn't cost us very much. In fact, appreciative speech rather than cynical speech opens the way for less personal depletion. Instead of constantly whining about how bad things are, we talk about how good things are. Instead of declaring environmental doom, we speak of environmental enchantment. We mean the words "How great thou art," but we also know the second verse, "How small we are." Our souls connect the two in thought and action. The point is to anticipate goodness. To become tough doves we change our language, which then changes our attitude. We ask for people to tell us more. We learn to appreciate what they say and don't say, what we see and don't see.

The capacity to be an intercessor is another strong approach to conflict. One night our dinner guests' kids were swimming in our pool. The neighbor kids threw rocks at them. They were jealous at hospitality to others and not to them. Our guests were frightened and huddled with their children inside. One of us went out and talked to the neighbor kids. Did they want to come in for a swim? Did they want to apologize to the children they had "bombed" before doing so? The answer to both questions was yes.

Our guests had a great time talking about their own parents as the evening progressed. One said, "My parents would have beaten the . . . out of me if I had thrown rocks." Another said, "My parents would have never let me play with kids who were my enemies." There are many kinds of intercessions. Some are godly, some are not. Some open doors, create possibilities, move toward appreciation; others close doors and make sure the rocks keep coming. Tough doves find situations all day long in which fight and flight are the normative response. We offer alternatives: we tend and befriend.

Tough doves listen, appreciate, intercede, link, and hope. We also get stuck. Our strategies don't always work brilliantly. Whether it is genetic engineering, abortion, pulling the plug, making peace, raising the minimum wage, keeping kids from blowing up their schools, or something simpler like organizing a family reunion, we humans find a lot of difficulties strewn on our soiled red carpet. We get weak. Our middle name is "thwarted." The good that we would do, we cannot do. The evil that we would not do, we do. We want to be tough doves—serious proponents of peace—but often we look like dead birds, legs akimbo on the soiled red carpet of our lives.

While we are weak, God is strong. Even Job understood, against his own evidence, that God in the end will be victorious. Nothing can separate us from the love of God, including nuclear disaster, bird flu, bad choices, and the failure to fill out our living wills correctly. Lyndon Johnson said to Martin Luther King: "Martin, you go on out there now and make it possible for me to do the right thing." Many of us are more blockers than quarterbacks in the great war for peace and justice. We help others do things. Football fans know that no offense manages without good blockers. Even in dumb meetings and sideline conversations, we can be blockers. We can speak up when hate enters the conversation. We can refuse to nominate known neurotics to positions of power in our churches. We can question authorities at school, home, bank, and stadium. When you feel like speaking up, speak up. Open your mouth. If out of fear you didn't speak, write a letter and say what you should have said when you didn't say it. Repent of your silence.

I think of fights of an intimate nature. Often we just shift the burden back and forth. Your fault, his fault, not my fault is the language of love at war. Tough doves are prepared to assume the burden and the responsibility (not fault but responsibility) for what they may have done "wrong." We don't avoid burdens, we assume them. We bear the burden. We pay from our extravagant budget line called love. We go further than we can. We have a need to offer sacrifices every day. The next time you say, "It is not my fault," change direction. Say instead, "This is my responsibility." See what happens.

Conflict may be inevitable in the art of doing good and living well. What is not inevitable is how we respond. We have an entire arsenal for peace. We ask to hear more. We listen. We appreciate. We intercede for others. We become football blockers for the good. We sacrifice. We spend our full budget down. Mostly we see conflict as our friend; we see conflict as the route to human transformation. Sometimes we are so glad to see conflict come our way that we are relieved at its arrival. So glad, sometimes we start to hum.

Tough doves know that we are not going to be victorious in every conflict. Instead, we think we are going to be graceful in defeat and graceful in our gladness. We are not going to let the perpetuity of conflict get in our way of living well and doing good. We are going to become the opposite of being afraid of conflict. We are going to be glad at its arrival. The practical ways to deal with conflict begin and end with humor.

I have often run an end-of-the-year contest for the largest mistake in the office. Such expectation of trouble defuses conflict by anticipating it. One of the entries was the typo in the first line of the first stewardship letter. "Here we give you *bead* for your journey and wine for your joy." Most people would prefer bread for their journey but no, not us.

We give the congregation beads for its journey and wine for its joy and ask them to offer donations for the bead. Another entry was the time that some pornography was inadvertently sent to half the congregation whose mailing list we had. Someone pushed the wrong button on their computer, hoping to delete it—or so they said—and sent it to one of our longer mailing lists. The rest was history. We are still braced for the first complaint—and now have more reason than ever to wonder if members of this parish read their email. A third entry had to do with laundering underwear in the nursery school, and I will spare you the details. When we anticipate conflict, we take away its power.

Once I worked with a secretary in a two-person office at a college chapel. She and I had a deal. The first five "disasters" of the day we would take in stride. On the sixth one we would flip out. This little daily liturgy turned us into tough doves, people who could manage what came our way—or at least manage some of what came our way. We became people who anticipated both success and failure and did so with humor.

The story of the flight to Egypt is a story that rounds up successes and failures. Mary and Joseph have gotten through their first crisis. As we know, there will be many more. They found a place to lay the baby's head. They were able to receive the gifts of the wise. Their worst mistake? Not staying home when the baby was due. Their worst success? Not understanding just how threatening the gifts from the wise were. It's nice to get gifts from the wise, isn't it? To get all A's on our report card? Or to end the year with money in the bank? Or to actually work-out the three days a week we said we would and to have seen the pounds slip away? Almost any success is a gift from the wiser part of us and our community. Success is a completion of a process. We said we would lose weight and we did. We said we would do well in school and we did. We get the gift not only of the grades or the improved health—we also get the approbation of the wise. Gold, frankincense, and myrrh arrive with the success.

The only problem with success, as many of you know too well, is that we are condemned to repeat it. It may be that successful people need to make mistakes as much as they need to achieve and hoard success. That's how learning happens. Without the risk involved in, let's say a flight to Egypt or a flight from Egypt, our very giftedness can become captivity. Our very success can become a prison. We can burn out by becoming the captives of our successes. When we anticipate lives of peace and peace only, we become tough on ourselves. When we anticipate lives commingled with peace and anxiety, success and failure, we become people who can truly manage the peace that comes their way without being condemned by it.

One of the most threatening comments made at my former church in Miami was made by a long-term lover of that congregation. He said, "I wonder if Coral Gables Congregational Church is strong enough to hold its gifts." We were having diversity troubles, which any congregation as diverse as ours is supposed to have. If we were true to our claim to be the most racially and economically diverse organization in town (a claim that was statistically accurate, by the way), then indeed we were meant to have diversity problems. Are we strong enough to hold our gifts? Do we expect trouble? Do we anticipate conflict? Do we embrace it, toughly and tenderly?

As individuals, many of us face the same challenge. Are we strong enough to hold our gifts? Were Mary and Joseph strong enough to hold their gifts? Look what happened to them. Their very giftedness, the fact that they were the vessel for the Messiah, got them into a lot of trouble—and that very quickly. We don't have to worry about whether these two young and gifted people were having burnout or encore anxiety. They didn't get to do the same thing over even once! They had to keep coming up with new skills. First shelter the baby, then show the baby off, then fly to Egypt, then flee from Egypt. First shelter, then adventure, then shelter, then more adventure.

Linda Immune, the Philippine educator, says that the very process of education is obtaining enough security to have an adventure. Then the adventure is to restore the security, which security must be abandoned on behalf of more adventure. In this context, we might even say that success understands when to go to Egypt and when to leave Egypt. We might even sing the old song, "Know when to hold it, know when to fold it." There is an Egypt to which we go and an Egypt from which we escape. How do we know when to do which? We are warned by our dreams, upheld by our gifts, but not captive to them. Nor are we captive to Egypt. We can leave whether or not Pharaoh gives us permission. We have freedom of movement in and out of Egypt—people who live well and do good are in fairly constant motion. When you embrace conflict, you say goodbye to Egypt and hello to freedom, the freedom to dream and to realize dreams.

Finally, those who know there is no life without some conflict are prepared for sacrifice. Jesus offers a different kind of sacrifice—the *sacer ficio,* or holy act of love. He doesn't need to burn animals or pay dues. But I am a small fan of a little sacrifice. Of being prepared for sacrifice. Tough doves know that their toughness and their doveness are expensive. They cost. And we write a personal budget that is ready to pay. If we go far toward sacrifice, we end up being self-righteous prigs. However, why do we have a feast budget if we are not willing to spend it from time to time?

 CHAPTER 5

SIMPLIFYING DOMESTICITY

When my former mother-in-law got a mixed reading on a mammogram, she went home and cleaned out all the drawers in all the dressers in her house. I remember being shocked. I thought Mary had become a bit loony and it took me a while to realize that she was just becoming more deeply herself. She was what we used to call a house-wife: a terrible word, but an identity nonetheless that she enjoyed fundamentally. Her idea of a good day was feeding people well. She would make a potato salad in the morning and consider that joy. If a big crowd was coming for dinner, she loved nothing better than making a large Manhattan-style clam chowder with clams fresh from the bay that surrounded her Long Island life. The tomatoes for the chowder could come from her garden. When she set the table for the chowder feast, she had freshly ironed napkins and a clean tablecloth. The bowls were sturdy and white and ample: they gave good meaning to the part of the word "liberal" that means generous. Generous, liberal, ample, large—these were the words that described a blessed domesticity.

Most remarkably, she enjoyed this life. She was a housewife before home economics was a required subject in school and after women had the freedom not to work outside the home. She lived a narrow historical window, one now long gone, probably never to return. Housing prices and other large-scale economic issues now require two incomes. Feminists may think we caused the change from Mary Schaper's way of life into something more liberating. But I don't think so. Home economics changed: one income was possible to sustain a family for only a brief window after World War II. Now, whether you want to make clam chowder and grow tomatoes or not, you must also work outside the home.

When Mary worried about what people would find in her dresser drawers were she to die, she really worried. She had an identity that had to do with domestic order and beauty. Very few men or women can afford that identity today. When we say, "My house is a mess," we mean it. One of the casualties of the new home economics is a gracious domesticity. We have become a people who work to have homes in which we can barely live. Long commutes and long workdays join with errands and kids' soccer games to keep most people out of their homes twelve or more hours a day. Why bother cleaning a house you are not going to live in?

There are answers to that question and they go to the heart of living well and doing good. People without a home-base are not good travelers. People without a place they call home are homeless. People who are homeless are likely to be afraid to challenge authority, afraid for their futures, afraid of just about everything. People who are afraid are not good citizens, especially not good democratic citizens, whose nobility requires time, study, conversation, and participation. When work takes over even family life, fewer and fewer people give a damn about the polis.

Only heroes can do that—and even heroes get tired of dirty sheets, dirty dishes, unrecycled recycling, and plants that have died for lack of water. In fact, today's home economics require people to be heroic multitaskers, and that finally devolves into dresser drawers in which we put whatever is at hand. Again, when we say our "house is a mess," we mean it.

People who try to improve the world from a house that is a mess are people who are off-base. Think about that concept, "off-base." We are standing on sand. We are standing on air. We are not sleeping on earth or on a foundation. We are discombobulated. Unbalanced. Off-base.

People who are on-base are people who are at home. Instead of being spiritually homeless and spiritually hungry, we are spiritually at home and spiritually well-fed. There is a real difference between an activist with a base and an activist without a base—and I'm not just talking politically. People with a base, people who are not threatened by their drawers or closets, attics or cellars, are at home. They feel like they belong to the universe instead of being an exile. We work so hard to pay our mortgages and then we don't enjoy what they buy. We mess it up.

Tidiness is not the only casualty that comes with neglected homemaking. Another casualty is beauty; another is health. Beauty of an aesthetic nature comes from the happiness of picking out your own curtains or bedspread or towels. It comes from caring about things like that. Health comes from caring about what you eat and how you eat it. A home that is not also hearth is unhealthy and ugly. How many activists try to improve a world when their own homes are unhealthy and ugly? Who are we kidding?

Tidiness is not just an external ring in the labyrinth. It is not an "out there" but an "in here" as well. When we are spending any time at all describing ourselves as cluttered or unkempt, we are wasting energy. Worse, we are feeding ourselves negative energy in a world where the positive is a life-and-death matter. Once negative energy enters the personal system, it infects a lot. Attitude *is* everything. Having a bad attitude about our homes can quickly lead to having a bad attitude about ourselves. That is not a very good position from which to improve the world. It too quickly turns to a guilt trip.

Magazines about homemaking abound. I think they get more popular the less time we spend at home. At least we can read about what might be while we are "out." Being "in" is such a foreign concept in so many ways that we prefer fantasized outs to real ins. I suspect that this fear of the "in" has spiritual consequences as well. We are what we are outside where we at least dress and present ourselves as people with a base. Most of us at least continue to dress well, even if the clothes we put on were recently on the bathroom floor.

What follows are a few ways to create a home when home-lessness is our economic commandment. First of all, we can remember Mary's joy, the way she made her kitchen a support group, health club, counseling center, day care center, and cooking class. How do we find her joy? I can give you her German potato salad recipe and you can remember with me how much she loved making it. Now, as people who buy all these services and more, as people who buy the potato salad in a plastic container, we might remember with respect how good an economy is where one salary or two half-salaries or even three halves for two people is enough. We might become people capable of economic imagination. Being negative about homemaking doesn't help us question the economy that has destroyed it. Instead, we might be imaginatively positive about what men and women might do in homes they make together, with work they can manage outside, with joy in the possibility of raising our own children, growing some of our own food, cleaning our own houses, being mentally well and supporting each other rather than buying all our services with jobs we can't stand. Instead, as feminists, we might object to women becoming more like men and insist on a world and an economy where men also become more like women.

Second, between now and the utopia I just described, we can get a handle on our homes. We can develop simple ways of taking care of them in ways that give us satisfaction and liberate us from the cute but ugly secret that our houses are a mess. I use a quadrant method. Each day I care for or appreciate a corner of one of the seven rooms in my house. I garden the same way. I don't like a day when I haven't done something to touch my house, even if it is no more than removing one cobweb, dusting one sill, cleaning one tablecloth, adjusting one picture frame. I don't like a day when I don't pull a few weeds or take care of some of the dirt on which my home lives. Even taking out the compost can matter to me. Here in New York we carry the compost we have frozen to the farmer's market. It gives me great joy to not throw it out.

This quadrant method also allows Tuesdays to be given to taking the garbage out and having it be a blessing instead of a bother. I work two-plus jobs; so does my husband. We don't have time to house-clean or home-make. But we make the time in very small intentional ways. We believe in our home. We like it. Some Sundays, we just take a tour of the house and appreciate the objects. Other times we declutter, wondering how in the world that corner could have become so filled up with stuff we don't need. My favorite bookstore has as its motto: "Books you don't need in a place you can't find." Houses have a way of becoming that way. When we confess, admit, rejoice that we need a base or we are no good outside, we find the time and way to care for our space.

A third way to think about domesticity in ways that affirm our need to live well and do good, to be inner and outer people at the same time, is to learn about *feng shui,* a Chinese art of appreciating place. *Feng shui* means a lot more than the composite of the spiritual environment, but we can start there to define it. *Feng shui* is simply the spiritual experience of a place, materially communicated. *Feng shui* is a loving of our nest, a loving of our shell. It is an appreciation of domesticity. It is an awareness that we live in a place. We do not live in *no*place; we live in *some*place.

A home can be spiritually beautiful from the inside looking out, as we'll describe in the internal clues which follow, or it can be beautiful from the outside looking in. Are trees visible from the center? Are there plants or flowers? Are there stones or fire pits? Is there water? What will the place look like in the next season and in all four of the seasons? Do you have a short view or a long view from the center? In Zen terms, where do you get enough horizon to be peaceful? Is the house cluttered or pleasingly spaced? Does it say to us that it is "small" or "large"? Do people seem to be proud of the space or ashamed of it? How much litter is there? How many benches are there? In other words, are people expected to sit and *be* in this place, or just move through and move on?

I think of a prank that MIT students pull off each year, in which they hold a contest to find out what outrageous gimmick can be brought to fruition on the campus. One year a police car was suspended from atop the main building on campus. Two dummies in uniform were placed in the front seat, drinking coffee and having donuts. This animation and suspension brought the hidden place out. It was fun because it combined the "attic" and the "campus," the up and down of the place.

In *feng shui* the matter of active chaos (mess) and passive chaos (old mess) is important. In a house there are usually many places where people feel comfortable enough to toss their clothes and books and papers around. *Feng shui* advises that this chaos-making needs to be in real time—as opposed to old and stale and never picked up. I think of the Berenstain Bears talking about "messy build-up" or the archaeology of an uncared for home. Looking for the pleasantness of the casual chaos and "mess" is a key to understanding a home. Where do people get to actually live and be? When I speak of the importance of being tidy, internally and externally, I do not mean without mess. I do not mean picked up. I mean a beautiful mess. Do people care about that space? How do they care for it?

Chi is enhanced by the presence of plants and animals, art, color, water, flowers, lighting, even mirrors. *Chi* is lost in a place where these things are not present. Unfortunately, way too many homes are sterile and institutional. How? By not including energy softeners in their place.

In a home the front door is considered the primary mouth of *chi*. All other doors are smaller mouths or openings. Where is the front door of the house? What are the doors like through which we will walk? I think of the great gate at Berkeley as an example of very positive *feng shui*. It opens beautifully and people rush through.

Feng shui doesn't only look inside at spaces in the plural. It also looks at space in the singular. Literally, *feng shui* means wind and water. How water does or doesn't surround or even exist on a campus is a crucial factor to its spiritual environment.

The location of a space, a private space or a public space, is crucial. *Feng shui* practitioners walk a land to find an auspicious location. They look for good soil and strong singing birds. They look for water and for elevation that catches the wind. Thus, homes sited on water are already somewhat automatically going to rate high in *feng shui* or spiritual beauty. Likewise, aquariums and fountains—adding water to land—are highly valued by people who appreciate *feng shui*. They bring the water in. Whenever I look at a house, I look out its windows. This border between the inside and the outside will be a key feature to the *chi* of a place.

Feng shui generalizes the questions of the spiritual composite of a place. In these places, do we feel calm or comfortable? Do we feel pleased? Is our eye intrigued? Do we want to know more about the place or less? Where are we drawn? Where would we sleep? Eat? Go if we were upset? Go if we were ecstatic? Have fun?

Once our sense of the beauty of a place is established, internally and externally, once we feel at home in our place, we are able to manage small and large tasks with appreciation. Even balancing a checkbook can be a Benedictine act: we did spend this money on this house and home and on these groceries and these meals. We did not spend the money on something that is not us. We spent the money on something that *is* us. Rather than being alienated from our checkbook, we might come to treasure it and the little math it makes us do from time to time.

Finally, I want to name the importance of lighting fires in a home. That may mean something as simple as accompanying our evening meal with a candle, or something as large as a bonfire outside. The most precious possession in our Amherst farmhouse is a large wired scale, salvaged from a duck farm that was giving way to a Wal-Mart in Riverhead, New York. The scale was used many years ago to weigh ducklings. We now use it as an outdoor fireplace. There was no question how to bid farewell to this farm when we moved to New York. We needed a big bonfire with the neighbors gathered round, even though we had to shovel the snow out of the scale to do the winter solstice fire. Our house was beautiful that night. Beauty is important to the activist. It makes us alive where we live.

These four directions can help us make a house a home. Simple plans to keep our house clean and clear join Mary's joy, which is a form of *feng shui*. From there we light and sustain fires, large and small. From there we keep our checkbooks. We can appreciate a home. We can take care of things in small and simple ways. We can learn to think of places as having spiritual qualities. We can become amateur *feng shui* artists. When we have a home, we are able to go out and take risks in the world. When we don't have a home, we will not be able to sustain risk-taking behaviors. We will shut down and in.

 CHAPTER 6

SIMPLIFYING CHILDREN

Our job is to light the flame in our children and send them out into the world—the imperfect world where, like us, they will also imperfectly parent. Our job is to watch when their fires smolder and threaten to go out—and to keep them alive by keeping ourselves alive. We neither oppress our children with our own failures, nor do we ask them to be who we were not or to achieve our own immortality through them. We did name our Katie "Katie Emma" for Emma Goldman, and we did name our Jacob "Jacob Frederick" for Frederick Douglas and our "Isaac Eugene" for Eugene Debs. We put heavy packs on their backs and in their names. We did want them to take the torch when our lights went out. They know that and are both impressed and oppressed by it. When the time is right, we hand them the heavier pack and hike on.

In *The Prophet,* the writer Kahlil Gibran understands this situation of the generations and more when he says:

Your children are not your children. They are the sons and daughters of life longing for itself. They come through you but not from you, and though they are with you yet they belong not to you.

You may give them your love but not your thoughts, for they have their own thoughts. You may house their bodies but not their souls, for their souls dwell in the house of tomorrow, which you cannot visit, not even in your dreams.

You may strive to be like them, but seek not to make them like you. For life goes not backward nor tarries with yesterday.

You are the bows from which your children as living arrows are sent forth. The Archer sees the mark upon the path of the infinite, and bends with you that your arrows may go swift and far. Let your bending in the Archer's hand be for gladness.

Kibran's remarkable words tell us that we are not the center of the universe, nor is our family, and that we dare not create our family as the center of our universe because we are part of the world, the future. That is the good news about families. It is so simple we can hardly ever get it right: we persist in imagining ourselves center stage when we are not. Thus we overdo parenting, overdo our sense of responsibility for our children, and overfunction as parents. Yes, there are exceptions, but most people I know are overinvolved with their children. One man said of his daughter's freshman math course at Yale: "We are having a little trouble with math." We use our children to become the selves we are not. Better we should become a self to which our child can relate, look up to, and imagine as a friend. Better we become a parent who is willing to age and change, succeed and fail in full sight of our children. Carl Jung argued that we must become anything and everything we want our children to become. Children learn by imitating; why teach them how to raise their own children as the selves they failed to become? Why teach children overfunctioning in the first place?

I know an extremely gifted family of four (doctor, lawyer, precocious children) used to doing everything well, who for many years took adventure trips—hiking, kayaking, climbing, and the like. But one year the whole family had to be evacuated a little short of the hundred-mile mark, going down the Appalachian Trail. With his arthritic hips and her "bad" feet they could not keep going. When their willpower was overcome by their bodies, after they had symbolically traded packs with their offspring, getting the younger ones to carry the heavier packs, they had no choice but to call for help. Knowing and loving this family, I could only imagine how hard this was but couldn't help thinking this was the best thing that could have happened to them. A little failure goes a long way. Why not set high ideals, like the Appalachian Trail, and also fail to complete the mission?

In the meantime, we raise our children by our delight in them. My children are long gone but I still know how to reverence the joy of a child. A little boy called Hardy came over one night and his spirit remains under the hassock in the center of our living room. Hardy immediately "got" the value of the hassock. First of all, it centered the room and that was where he wanted to be. Second, the cat hides under it and the skirt lifts up. Hardy played most of the evening with the cat under the hassock. He lifted the skirt, he laughed. He put the skirt down, he laughed. The cat was not amused and did not appreciate the attention but did not budge for about two hours, offering a form of babysitting that here in New York often costs a pretty penny. When the cat disappeared and Hardy lifted the skirt to find nothing there, he wailed, he ran away, he cried, he screamed, he jumped up and down. Maybe he too was overreacting and overfunctioning—who knows?—and his misery at the cat's disappearance was equal only to his joy at the cat's presence. We are so lucky to have child energy in our house, as are our other friends, and to know how to value it. Living well while doing good is also about retaining our capacity to appreciate the young, the childlike, and the simple.

I would like to say that I raised my children by the art of sheer joy in them, but I did not. I worried about their manners and the way they mis-kept their rooms, and once cried in a long-remembered family incident when my eldest came home with his first C in math. He was brilliant in math. He was also bored by the teacher. One of the biggest mistakes I ever made in parenting was not to trust him when he told me that his sixth-grade teacher was depressed. We had just moved to Amherst and I thought he was just having an "adjustment" problem, but he had diagnosed her absolutely correctly. He got the C in math because she was so down and so boring. I didn't trust what he said about her—and the rest is expensive private school history. When it comes to overreacting and overfunctioning, I know my way around.

So I want to go on record that I wish I had enjoyed them more and shaped them less, trusted them more and doubted them less. I also go on record against the cliché that grandparents have all the fun and none of the responsibility. Perhaps parents could learn to have fun while having responsibility? Is that too idealistic? I think not. I think both parents and children miss the joy when responsibility edges out glee. When the cat skips out from under the hassock and the child flips out, we miss one of the great scenes of the play if we don't pay deep attention. Most parents enjoy the joke that goes, "I'm so broke I can't even pay attention." Our sense of deep scarcity and fear makes us try too hard. If we try less hard, we can lift the skirt on the hassock—and lift the veil on childhood. We can see deeply into the child's eyes and borrow their joy for our own. There is not even interest to be paid, in money terms—only in the terms of paying attention, showing interest, acting involved.

The clue to raising children well may be looking at them from the point of view of their grandparents, because "short-term-itis" is the biggest problem for people of activist bent. We imagine ourselves at the center of the universe. We are properly accused of being "anti-family values," a concept so distorted that it needs the kind of unpacking an attic gets. Finally, we imagine we are in charge of the world's improvement and forget that we came from parents and we go to children, that we came from a gaseous cosmic explosion and return to dust and ash. Let me go at each of these issues, slowly.

When people who want to live well and do good consider having children, they often see them as deficits. Children will take the time and money we need to save the world. They will turn us into responsibility machines. They will cause us to be conservative. Indeed, having children will do all of these normal, good things. Simultaneously, children are enormous assets: they cure us of "short-term-itis" and thinking, falsely, that we are the center of the world. Without children we might turn selfish on global warming. Once children are on the scene and in our hearts, we become vicious about our children's picnics in 2047. In that year, I will be one hundred years old. I will probably be dead, but if I am not I would surely like to be wheeled or hauled to a picnic near my proposed gravesite and there to breathe clean air and look at clear water. If I have to wear a gas mask to that picnic, I will not be happy. And I will be unhappy less for myself than for my children. How dare my car driving habits take their air? How dare the lack of global leadership spoil their water?

Do-gooders are prisoners of their own self-consciousness as long as they imagine themselves uni-generational. There is no such thing: we are all multigenerational beings. We come from parents, we go to children—biological as well as social beings—and even if we don't reproduce ourselves, we reorient the human gene pool simply by removing ourselves from it. We are part. We are not whole. The most remarkable thing that Charles Darwin said is that "all things are related." We have relatives, in air, water, sky, and sea. We have relatives in each other and in chimpanzees and in turtles and in fish.

When it comes to family values, and those on the Religious Right who see the 1950s as their peak, we can have a field day. We can move out of the prison of one historical era, one postwar economic boom, one version of family, and go into the great memory of matriarchies and patriarchies of the past, the great historical vitality of different family values and practices deserving the utmost reverence. When the Religious Right insults the open religious groupings with accusations of being anti-family, the only proper response is a humble smile. No, the nuclear family is not God. It is short-term. When it is deep in defensive self-consciousness, it is an affront to God, not an imitation of God.

Families help us understand family values as our family plus the world family. Grandparenting is the lens through which we can see both of these things. When we look at our families as grandparents, we see that we are not the center of the world. We see that family values have great strengths and great limits, and that even something as good as valuing our family can become distorted by short-sightedness. We also see that we are part of a long line of generations and that liberates us from our children for our children. We put a hassock in the middle of the room—and other people's children enjoy it as well.

There is not one model of being in family. We can live deep in the truth that we might and may be different. Having children gives activists the gift of right-sizing our hopes, of living in our history and not some fantasized center of the universe. Children help sustain our virtue and activism; they do not hamper it. They give it and us the depth we both need. It is foolish to ask the question, "How can we have children in a world like this?" The real question is, "How can we *not* have children in a world like this?" People who want to save the world need children to keep them humble, alive, connected, and soft.

When our family grew to three children, Warren and I had to move from "man-on-man" to a zone defense. Our first was born when I was thirty-six, and then twins when I was thirty-eight. We knew we needed help and we got it. We resisted day care because it felt like the commoditization of parenthood—we cleaned our own house, cooked our own food, and didn't like paying for the services of domesticity. We also resisted day care because I couldn't part with my children. I had a bonding issue that was absurd in feminist terms, but not in mine. I could not let them go. My concern was that I would squeeze them to death in the beginning. I thought I would fail them by putting their fires out in the name of mine for them.

Finally, after much worry and therapy, we got lucky and found a "third" partner to help us raise the children. Her name is Nancy, and she came to us one day from heaven. She lived with us for fourteen years and we never knew how that happened, but she said one day, "Can I take your kids to the park someday?" and I said, "Yes." She is our nanny, aunt, friend, sister. Our kids love her. She gave Warren and me the freedom to be activists.

Does every couple want a third around at meals? No. But no matter what solution we find, admitting that the 1950s version of family, even with its great press and its enormous public relations staff, doesn't work in a world where grandmothers live at a distance and everyone works is a start. Just admit it. In fact, many parents become activists on behalf of a different kind of world precisely because the nuclear family is such a beast. We are horribly lonely in a world of Mom, Dad, and two kids, especially when one or both parents has to commute an hour or more a day. The world is not set up for this; there is a cultural lag afoot in our generation, where the world of work is in major conflict with the presumed virtues of calm and lengthy parenting. American children are among the most neglected in the world—unless we have lots of money to pay for their lessons, soccer, pickups, and drop-offs. Without that, the kids and their Game Boys and television sets are pretty much on their own. I know: I used *Sesame Street* and other videos with abandon. They were my only way to get a moment's peace.

When I think of the huge number of single parents trying to do what I just described as difficult for three of us, I wince. Margaret Mead's notion of a "starter marriage" without children is a good one. Everyone has two marriages: one while young, without children, another when older, with children. It could be used wisely to keep people from marrying and having children too young. It pays attention to the anthropology of the moment, anthropology being the link between economics and culture. Both have changed since my own childhood. When it comes to family life, living well and doing good starts with an analysis of how and why things have changed. We need to value the family that is, not the one of nostalgic fantasy. The real world is constantly changing: one model may suit for now, another for the next century. The idea that there is something called "normal" is nearly impossible to imagine.

When it comes to the social arts of activism and the human arts of living, we can learn much more from our failures than we can from our success. I am often reminded of the fight I got into with my first child's kindergarten teacher. This teacher was brilliant when she gave Isaac a bad grade on one of his first reading projects. Why? "If I don't give him a bad grade early, he won't experience failure early enough and then he won't know what hit him when he is eighteen and the world is no longer his oyster." She was right: failure can sometimes be a better teacher than success.

On the other hand, children need to have successes in order to have a healthy sense of self-esteem. I remember when our boys, at ages six and eight, managed to deliver a baby goat when we got home late to our small farm in Riverhead, New York. Our goat's name was Angelina Grimke, named for one of the two famous South Carolinian feminists, and when she went into labor, the babysitters from next door lost it. Somehow Isaac and Jacob got a hold of a blue *New York Times* wrapper and pulled the baby goat out together. I think of it as one of their finest moments. (I think of it as one of my not-so-fine moments. I trusted those babysitters way too much!) Children not only need to learn failure; they need to learn success. They need to learn how to cope in a world where Mom and Dad are often late. I shiver when I think of how this story could have been different: my absence, the babysitters' incompetence (which I should have known), the goat's advanced pregnancy could have combined to give my boys a terrible failure. Raising children is coming to know the great value of luck.

We often get compliments on our three children these days, and they are indeed doing well. When people say that awful cliché about the apple not falling far from the tree, I interrupt vigorously. I love the compliments but I also know how much the success of our kids is due to sheer luck. I know many parents who have worked and loved and hoped and done as much as we have. They have been superb parents, and with very different consequences. Parenting is a whole lot of luck and a whole lot of love—and a whole lot of culture lag, working against us.

Getting the combination of self-esteem and self-assessment right is one of the great gifts of parenthood. I think very few of us ever do; I think all of us try. These skills of confidence and humility balance well in strong adults. Maybe we have children so they can teach us—God knows we teach them, even what we don't want to. I watch my children imitate my strengths and my weaknesses—and I just want to hide. I watch myself fold the dishtowels exactly the same way my mother folded dishtowels—and I just want to hide. I watch my shoulders bend the same way my father's shoulders bent—and I just want to hide. We are part of a long line, front and back, and we are the great-grandparents of the future. That is what it means not to be the center but to be the spoke in the wheel of a great and glorious universe. Every posture, every little thing we do is picked up by the universe through our children. If, right now, we are ignoring our own parents or complaining about them, we can bet our children are noticing.

I have often joked that I have raised "free-range children." I wanted them to grow themselves as much as be grown by me. I have been extraordinarily neglectful as a parent, keeping up a full-plus work schedule and a full-plus life. My kids are free to say: "I missed you, I would have wanted more of you, I wish you had been home more, I wish you hadn't been so restless, I wish we hadn't moved so much." These remarks hurt, but they are also right. Children teach us who we are. They are very aware of who we are, warts and all.

This great sense of humility and failure can keep us alive enough to live well and to try to do good. Our children may be the ticket to both. Joy in their being—including joy in their frankness—will place us in right relationship to both the universe and ourselves. That relationship is small, but significant precisely because it is small.

As I write, our twins are now twenty-one and ready to graduate from college; our oldest son is twenty-three and will get married this year. I am entering the year in which I will turn sixty; I will celebrate my twenty-fifth wedding anniversary. In the twinkling of an eye, our children have grown and all but gone. My nest is as empty as my heart is full. All those sunrises, all those sunsets, all those goats, and all those teachers. So many Frisbee games, soccer games, softball games, school plays, report cards, boyfriends and girlfriends, ins and outs, ups and downs! Where did they go? The key to parenting is in this fragile, fleeting, joyous reality.

Kahlil Gibran was right when he talked about children being the arrows we shoot into the world. Our children also live to pick up our packs when we get tired of carrying them. They live for us the way we live for them. We want them to be good parents and good grandparents, and also good children when we are too old to hike. It makes for a beautifully centered universe. When we neglect our own parents on behalf of our children in the great "sandwich" period, we are really showing our children how not to care for us, and instead to live their own lives through their own children. Family values means valuing the world family as well as our own. It means acting as grandparents all the time, those who keep the joy out ahead of the responsibility. The key is knowing when to trade the heavier backpack for the lighter one at just the right time, year after year, day after day.

 CHAPTER 7

SIMPLIFYING ROMANCE

R omance either breaks our heart or sustains it. In the area of intimacy more people fall and get broken than any other way. Our hearts once broken are less repairable than our arms or legs. Coming up with gloriously realistic expectations for romance is an art. It competes well with trapeze training.

Again the metaphors can help us balance our enormous hopes for love with our actual capacity to love. Not to *be loved,* but to love. We can have all the romance we can give, not less, not more. We pick up five sticks of expectations and leave the rest on the ground. We sustain romance, we don't let it be a shooting star that extinguishes our lighthouse. And we have a fine sense of tiny humorous lights about it: we are fireflies rather than flying by.

The eroticization of everyday life is one of the key solutions to the whole problem of living well and doing good. Even the language in my last sentence shows our original dilemma: I call living well and doing good "a problem." It is not a problem. It is a joy. It is a possibility. It is a matter of salting the everyday problems of living with a sense of beauty, aesthetics, sensuality, eros. Life has no flavor without these matters. When we add salt to everyday life, we eroticize it. We make it interesting to others and ourselves.

How do we do we salt the odd flavorlessness that comes into our lives uninvited? We value and prioritize our intimate relationships and work and play to make them fun. We choose beauty and fashion at table and in our clothes. We try to look good while being good. We dare to be angry and we dare to be passionate, excited; we don't soothe ourselves or calm ourselves down. We embrace beauty; we wear it and make it our own.

Those who want to live well and do good need look no further to make life interesting, vital, alive, and romantic than to eroticize everyday life. By making erotic I mean making beautiful, making amusing, making the deep sensuality of all things come to the fore and be noticed. Erotic is the spectrum from sensual to sexy, the line drawn between flat and enthusiastic affect. Erotic involves a lot more than coitus—although erotically alive people like that, too. Erotic means a range of behaviors. Flirting. Looking good. Paying attention to how we look. Walking as though we are beautiful, not trudging along. This is a low-cost form of personal entertainment. Nobody is against it and nobody charges us for it.

Being erotic is almost always the intentional making of a move on someone, asking a question that goes deeper than how the Mets did last night. We pry a little. We open up a little. We take risks. We make boredom our chief enemy and amuse others and ourselves as often as possible. Even if we have become someone others call "ugly"—too fat, misshapen, scoliotic, disabled, scarred—we can still be erotic because eros comes from the inside. Anyone of any shape and size can do it—even me, with a swayed back and an extra ten pounds. Tomatoes that get tossed because they aren't good enough to go to market still make a good sauce.

We find other ways to use ourselves and to bring out our beauty: we can wear a fake flower in our hair on the days when all we can imagine wearing is what we wore yesterday, our comfortable black jeans and the black shirt and the same old shoes.

Is there a way to sum up the eroticization of everyday life? Yes. Think of it as the constant interaction of four things. First, *intimacy,* in which we get close or try to get close to others most of the time. Then *beauty,* in which we search for the beautiful in every encounter, every person, in the subway, the garden, the bedroom, and the office. Third, *fashion,* by which we add unnecessary fluffs to our pillows and outfits and rooms. And finally, *excitement,* refusing to be bored and enjoying the calm that exists on the other side of excitement. Intimacy, beauty, fashion, and excitement: these eroticize everyday life. Everyone has the power to pay them heed, daily, hourly, weekly, monthly. I think of the Polish woman who escaped right before the Nazis arrived, along with her son and one suitcase. In it was all they needed, plus her lace tablecloth. Every night as they fled, she spread the tablecloth out. If she can spread lace in the middle of tyranny, I daresay we can make our normal lives erotic.

We can see a lime green scarf in a store and buy it for the woman friend we are having lunch with. Why? Because she will look great in it. Is such extravagance and gift-giving offensive in a world of poverty? Yes, it is. But refraining to take such little flights and jumps into the fun parts of life will not necessarily end poverty. Instead, it may end our spirit and that will affect our work with poverty.

Eroticizing, beautifying, accessorizing is a romantic strategy for living that goes beyond courtship and partnership, though it surely has a role in that too. Many activists think they are too serious and too important to enjoy the eroticism of partnership, but just the opposite is true. They are especially adept at partnership because their social analysis tells them they live in a throwaway culture. Staying committed to someone who develops mental illness or severe diabetes or Alzheimer's is an act of great love, a beautiful and deeply anticonsumerism activity. When we keep living well and doing good together, we partner beauty with commitment, romance with reality, as often as possible.

Let's consider intimacy first. Lots of people think that saving the world is such a serious enterprise that they shouldn't bother partnering or flirting with romance. Many argue that celibacy is the best route for a do-gooder. And it may be: at least when we are celibate we don't have our intimates angry with us all the time for having to compete with our virtue. My husband and children often say to me, "No need to go to the ballgame with us tonight, even though we have free tickets. You are going out with God again." I was deeply impressed when a new field-work student of mine turned down an opportunity to work on the first Friday night that he was on the job. He said, "I have taken Friday nights for my wife and me to be together. I am so sorry I can't do this event with you." He didn't really sound sorry at all. He sounded happy that he had developed a life rhythm of prioritizing his most intimate relationship. In four years of marriage he and his wife have not missed a Friday night yet. They have eroticized their week, their life, their relationship.

Another way to prioritize romance and passion is to keep ourselves and our spirit animated. It turns out that a new organization exists to allow people to try on other jobs so that for a week or so you daily get to be the person you fantasize being. You stop hooking your ladder to a building you don't want to climb and you stop working for health insurance. It turns out that the most desired job to try for a week is being an animator, someone who takes drawings and turns them into life. I was quite moved by the notion that what many working Americans want is "animation." So many of us are stuck in jobs that require us to withdraw the blood from our veins and go skeletal, put up with the dumbdown, the neckache, the backache, the robotic stare at the screen, the "Yes, sir" mode. When we think we can't take it anymore, we remind ourselves that we need the money, need the insurance, and seek animation in the few waking hours we have left after traveling to the job that drains us completely. We all face difficulties on our jobs, but even there we can remain animated. We can encourage each other. We can trust in a different kind of future. Lean toward it. Organize for it; demonstrate for it; link with the others who want the same thing. Wink your way through the day. Attach yourself to another kind of world and detach from the organization.

I was very moved by a poem by Joyce Greenberg Lott called "Maine Landscape" from her book of poems *Dear Mrs. Dalloway*. A wife notices her husband is setting the porch table with a cloth so she won't see the chipping paint. Then she notices that he has cut the grass. Then she sees a late fall spider web through the window from which she should not be watching. She defines this powerful moment as having "not to do anything but watch." I love the idea of a woman doing nothing but watching someone taking care of her. She has joined him in making a simple priority out of their romantic life. These two probably make beautiful love after nights like these—a kind of lovemaking that escapes those of us who won't "date" each other or cover over the chipping paint.

Once I was given a free massage, and the woman who worked on me had to instruct me over and over again that she and not I would be doing the lifting of my arm and my leg. When she would touch it, I would lift for her. She laughed: "Women, why are they always trying to help?" The experience of letting her lift me limb by limb was wonderful. I had laid my bucket of heavy water down. She was picking it up—ritually, of course—but what fun it was. Romance is surely about giving. It is also about receiving. It is a double motion. We give and receive and our partners give and receive, and wonderful things happen between us as a result.

I remember going to a very well-traveled and erudite friend's house and finding nothing on his walls or shelves. No *objects d'arte*. No paintings. No pictures. No nothing. No animation. I had to ask why. It turns out that after his divorce he put his share of the precious items from thirty years of travel into a storage center. Photos from Nice. A sculpture from Kenya. I could go on. When he moved, he either forgot to give the storage center his address or they lost it. Either way, he didn't pay the storage bill for three months. Then (isn't it funny how addresses can be found after they have been lost?) he got a check for $38.00. The storage center had sold his material life history and sold it by the pound. Whenever you think you don't have time to maintain an intimate relationship, imagine its loss. Imagine the cost of the loss. Make arrangements, pound by pound, to re-eroticize the relationship. You will be glad you did. You will also find the expense in time and energy in staying together much less than the time and expense of separating.

What happens too often in partnerships is that the fire goes out. Hyperactivity gets our twigs wet—or we just stop bothering. You can tell how intimate a couple is by how much they look at each other and how much they touch each other. In my life, I want the maximum intimacy with my life partner. I don't want it to get dull or stale. The slightest amount of flirting or engagement within the relationship makes me happy all day long. Days after we make love are twice as good as days where sleep has set in before touching and playing with each other. The very best part of my day is being held as I drift awake. Conversely, when things aren't going well between us, I am preoccupied with a debilitating sadness. Am I suggesting that intimacy and eros can keep us alive to the work of justice? Am I suggesting an instrumental relationship, that if we want to stay alive to the work of justice we should stay alive in a relationship? Yes, I suppose I am. Marriage, for me, has its own value beyond what joy it lets me bring to my work, but it is also richly connected to what I can do for others. The happier I am, the more work I can do. When I feel ugly or untouched, I feel unhappy with my work. Listlessness never sustained a political movement.

Staying romantically alive has to do with giving up calm on behalf of excitement. We are the ones who cause the dinner party to take off, who say outrageous things just to get the conversation going. One reason we may come to tolerate war and injustice is that we have let our erotic muscles go flaccid: we have lost the capacity to care intensely. If depression is anger without enthusiasm, and I think it is, many activists are just downright depressed. It shows in our own lack of enthusiasm for our own bodies. Indifference, flaccidness, and lack of passion: these are the results of letting love's fire go out between intimates.

Beyond life with our "significant other," there are many other ways to eroticize life. Flowers on the table, not eating from Styrofoam combine with a healthy glow and an agile body and spirit. Some days we should just wear a hat, or put on pink and orange together. Some days we should be late to meetings because we spent too much time getting dressed. When we care about things spiritual for a living and a life, we need the care of things material as a basis. When I went to Miami and only had Birkenstock sandals and corduroy pants (a fine uniform in western Massachusetts), I immediately purchased black patent leather Birkenstocks. I needed an upgrade.

Is it possible to be too concerned about face cream and patent leather, body shape and fashion? Of course. Is it possible to be too little concerned? You bet. Activists who intentionally look "different" from ordinary people will not find ways to say much to them. I remember a clergy friend of mine who was to call on a rich congregant on behalf of a joint project we were running. Since he rides a bike recreationally for long distances, he decided to bike to her house. The reason we didn't get the contribution we had carefully groomed him for? He was sweaty when he arrived. She was not impressed. Should she have been more broad-minded? Yes. So should he. He should have known that his appearance was going to matter to her. "You can't tell a book by its cover" is great folk wisdom, but in a world where interactions are multiplied and sped up, often we have just minutes to know each other. What we wear, how we carry ourselves, whether or not we are sweaty, matters a lot more in a speeded-up world. Many do-gooders seem to think that lack of attention to our bodies is a sign of virtue. It is time, in my opinion, that we put on a few feathers.

George Lakoff's book *Don't Think of an Elephant: Know Your Values and Frame the Debate* is on many of our minds because he advocates saying positively what you want—instead of opposing or whining. Say what you want. Work toward it. Reframe the debate. The Ghandian language of "become who you want the world to be" rings true in this context. When we look like who we want to be, we have already captured the initiative in any conversation. I used to think these things just mattered to women; I have learned through sons, husbands, and friends that they also matter tremendously to men. (Men just have less permission to talk about it.) Dressing our tables and ourselves is important to how we dress and frame our politics. When we put our bodies, our clothes, our skin, and ourselves at the center of it, and we stay there, we reframe the debate. Sometimes this can become manipulative—just as sitting with your partner at the breakfast table and saying, "I want to have more fun" is a tad manipulative when what you really feel is, "We don't get around much anymore." Nevertheless, deciding how to frame the pictures of our experience is crucial—and we can do better at it.

If I were to start one place with male activists, it would be with those who say, "I don't dance." I would move in on that excuse for self-protection and recommend that the non-dancers learn to dance. Why? Because dancing is sexy, that's why. Because it helps to escape the prison of self-consciousness, where what matters most is what others see in you, and move into the clearing where what matters is what *you* think of you. When we make ourselves beautiful, sexy, fashionable—or as much so as we can—we are not manipulating our image. We are taking care of ourselves. We are creating our creatureliness. We are behaving aesthetically, not politically. The reframing that is necessary for activists who have gotten dowdy understands consumerism, understands the book and its cover, values the inner without excluding the outer. Activists don't need to be afraid of beauty. We need to embrace it, wear it, and make it our own.

 CHAPTER 8

SIMPLIFYING SIZE

I have argued that living well and doing good are twins, flip sides of the same coin. Thus while doing good by staying fixed on the possibility of a new, different, and better world, we live well by making homes, having children, leading erotically interesting lives. We don't become extremists: we simply draw people to the power of our vision by living well, outside the well-advertised routes. We live enjoying the world of things and markets; we do not live as consumers but instead we live materially, well. Chic cheap? Maybe. We also live beyond ideology and refuse to force our points of view down other people's throats. We attract rather than persuade, witness rather than evangelize, act but do not force. We are drawn by the vision of a better world, and in thanksgiving for it we build small fires every day.

There is no point in pretending that these transformations of our way of being are easy. They are actually quite difficult because the transition is a turn that is small but very hard to make. It is almost as though we have flaccid back muscles and, instead of being able to look at the world from the grace side, we look at it from the effort side and just can't stop. Our back won't let our bodies turn: we don't have the muscles to make the small turn that would show all the difficulties as being less than they are. For example, war is huge. We should stop it. We also *may* stop it. It is the twist from *should* to *may* that matters. Poverty is huge. We should stop it. We also *may* stop it. Again, it is the twist from *should* to *may* that matters. This shift from *ought* to *can*, *should* to *may* is massive—and it is very small. How do you retrain a muscle? Inch by inch. Think of living well by doing good as physical therapy after you have broken your collarbone. It will come back. But it will come back by the steady accumulation of small actions. I am deeply inspired by the Native American understanding of how a tree falls: not by any one blow but on the one hundredth blow.

That strategy of using the small and steady to lever the large is the one I want to articulate here. It is turtle over hare, David over Goliath, little over big. The Japanese call it *kazen,* the art of small things. By that they mean arranging flowers as though we were reframing the whole world, a small bow that is almost invisible to the large earth. In Christianity, the closest thing is the story of the widow's mite. To the Temple treasury she quietly gives a small coin. Richer people loudly give large coins. The difference is magical to Jesus.

Another illustration: physical therapy retrains only one small piece of the muscle at a time. Some time ago I had to have eye therapy. My eyes suddenly split the view into two parallel pieces, which I thought was perfect for the Gemini that is me. After a while, though, it wasn't so funny. The eye doctor in Patchogue, New York, promised me that ten therapy sessions later, I would pull the world back together. Sure enough, weekly, I drove the thirty miles from Riverhead on the eastern end of Long Island into Patchogue, there to stare into a large steely machine for half an hour. I had to work on it, stare hard, and pull the brain into coordination with the eye. But it worked: the world returned to unity. That experience, as well as countless other experiences of turning huge tasks, like writing a book, into small, doable chunks, has taught me the value of the small. The idea of writing a whole book is impossible, but writing small parts of a book is not. Taking things down to small, bite-size portions is the strategy of the small. We can trust it—and we can even enjoy it. I learned to like the mornings going to Patchogue, picking out a few favorite places to reward myself along the way. They, too, taught me the value of the small.

I think God created the world in small batches, like the kind of jams and jellies local organic farmers make. Small-batch raspberry jam is better than large-batch. You can prove it yourself. Why else would creation be so filled with small, unnecessary pleasures like morning glories, spider webs, sushi, and frozen yogurt, just to name a few of my friends?

One way we can surely live well and do good is to teach our muscles, particularly our eye muscles, how to see the small and to enjoy it. We can be rich either by having great resources or by having small needs, according to William Sloane Coffin. The latter means a daily search for a spider web or sushi bar. We can train ourselves to think of our days as rich and full by seeing one small thing well, and seeing the unity of world and experience through it.

Let me tell you about an enchanted experience on the Fourth of July, 1976. I had picked up an elderly friend to go to a wedding in Scarsdale, but I was not in an enchanted mood about getting her at Newark and driving through all the traffic. For some reason, though, the traffic was easy and I had an impulse to drive across the George Washington Bridge. I also knew the tall ships were sailing up the Hudson, so even if we got stuck in traffic, we could see them. Well, the bridge was clear and the ships were sailing. Winifred, age seventy,

yelled, "Stop the car!" I did. She jumped out and started taking pictures, shouting "Wow!" and bouncing up and down.
A policeman came over fairly quickly: "Move, Lady." She
said something profane to him, he laughed his head off, and
she went on taking pictures.

There are just as many authorities in our heads, telling us
to move on. When it is time for us to view something beautiful, particularly if it is part of our program of noticing the
small, often we have to defy the authorities in order to survive.

Another night in Riverdale, 1992. A nor'easter in
December closed all the schools in Long Island where I was
living. I was teaching a class at the big convent there and
couldn't figure out whether to get home to the kids or stay
put. The radio said that the trains were out, the blizzard was
coming—and I was in a room with a view of the Hudson
River, my version of paradise. As the evening progressed,
large ship after large ship came up the river, fifty in all,
sparkling in my river, being moved out of the ocean. I was
once again enchanted, which means feeling large and small
and connected—an experience Sigmund Freud identified by
the term "oceanic"—all at the same time. "Enchante" say
the French when they meet one another.

Enchantment can come from grand forms of luck—like
mine during this nor'easter—or it can come from learning to
look at one boat at a time and enjoy it. Again we are engag-
ing a form of spiritual therapy that mimics the slow action
of physical therapy.

Yes, there is global warming and terrible suffering on the
streets of Calcutta. The Ganges is horribly polluted and so is
the Hudson, but people still jump into both to get things
that money can't buy. We may work all day and all night
long to save great rivers, great air, and this great earth, but
if we don't pause to enjoy what we are saving, all our effort
will do no good. In order to achieve large victories, we may
retrain ourselves to notice the small. The great feminist

writer Simone de Beauvoir is said to have worn a piece of string around one finger as a reminder to pay attention.

As a clergyperson, I often get involved in absurd situations. Yesterday a man called to request a baptism and I told him to come right over to discuss it. He said he couldn't, because he was photosensitive and it was too bright out. He called later in the day to say he could come Friday because the weather channel said it is going to rain. Again I said fine. Then he related a dream in which he was told he had to be baptized by a certain date, two weeks hence, so if it was too light on Friday, he would have to come next week, given his deadline. The conversation was clearly a little off and part of me wanted to tell him to go away. The other part of me said, "Donna, he is asking for baptism. Get real!" Anyway, the baptism is scheduled, I have invited a few congregants, and we will pour water, say prayers, and avoid the light. When things like this happen, as they do often enough, I am reminded of a phrase I learned in seminary, which frightens me: "The success of the intervention depends on the inner quality of the person doing the intervention." In other words, if I am not well, I probably won't do good. The addition of this baptism to the Friday schedule will create less time for spider webs, so I will have to be sure to reschedule my physical therapy-attentiveness sessions.

Instead of being released by the power of the small for the big, I am often troubled by the power of the small to keep me from getting to the large. Two problems plague most people I know, including me. One is short-term: the inability to get destiny or destination in place and to act from and toward it. The other is fuzzy goals. Because I don't know exactly what I want from today or tomorrow, or from you or me or us or them, I often behave non-strategically. I buzz along in a fuzzy framework of creeds, stories, scripts, theories, and ideologies. Some days end with me wondering why I moved that pile of papers from one side of my desk to another. What kept me from acting on at least two or three pieces of my "preposterous," the name my daughter gave at age nine to my kitchen counter? She had just learned the word and was looking for a perfect way to use it. She found it on the counter. All she could describe was the paper: she didn't see all the hidden scripted messages that were also there. She didn't see that the preposterous contained both sane and insane requests for baptism and that, to get real, I had to say "yes" to many of them. I did vow to stay well enough to do the baptisms right. I live in the narrow space between constant repentance and constant effort, and there I seek the salvation of the small and the spider's web.

Not to have the time or will to show up at the very physical therapy I know will save me is my sin. I *may* show up but I don't show up. And some days my short-term-itis joins up with my fuzzy goals and I mess around. I don't repent because I don't really think I have sinned. If I don't know where I am headed with my life and don't have distinct goals, I will probably be quite comfortable not knowing where I have gone wrong. Since I don't know what is right, I won't know what is wrong.

Still, both of my problems—fuzziness and short-term-itis—have a positive side. What happens as I fuzz and buzz along is often quite beautiful. Sometimes wonderful things find me. Serendipity—what you find that you are not looking for—is a magnificent experience. I remember very well the day I met a woman who has become a dear friend. On the day I met her at a business lunch, I had vowed not to make any new friends until I took better care of the ones I had. I had just received an angry letter from a friend about why I had not responded to her phone calls. But as Catherine revealed more of herself to me during the lunch, I just started to laugh. I was breaking my own promise within hours of making it.

While serendipity and aimlessness are magnificent things, they also get in the way of purpose. They keep us from the ritual retraining of our behavior that says we may and must pay attention to the small. They get in the way of art, too: the play we should be writing, the song we should be singing, the change we should be making, and the church we should be being. Strategy is good—and to behave strategically, we need to give ourselves over to something like a creed. A creed is a statement of belief, within or outside of a religious context, a mission statement, or a personal map. Christians use it to proclaim in a large way the map by which we may daily live. It is like a place of shade where we can hide from the heat of the sun. Or a thick rug under the living room furniture: we don't look at it much, but it is there, grounding us. I love the way the Masai people in East Nigeria rewrote the *Gem Na* creed in 1960 at their own council, called the Congregation of the Holy Ghost. It is a big statement, a big rug, a lot of shelter from the sun, a communal mission statement:

> We believe in One High God, who out of love created the beautiful world. We believe that God made good his promise by sending his Son, Jesus Christ, a man in the flesh, a Jew by tribe, born poor in a little village, who left His home and was always on safari doing good, curing people by the power of God, teaching about God and man, and showing that the meaning of religion is love. He was rejected by his own people, tortured and nailed hands and feet to a cross, and died. He was buried in the grave, but the Hyenas did not touch him, and on the third day he rose from the Grave.

From this creed they can live in small daily ways, well. We all need a destination. Often the small, which is our salvation,

91

requires the large to move us toward it. We need a large plan, which we then execute in slow and small ways. Otherwise we just get lost and wander. A personal mission statement keeps me somewhat protected and shaded from the hot sun of my one hundred years on the globe (if I am lucky); it also propels me intro strategic behavior.

Why is it important to step back and think strategically? Why is it important to have some kind of creed or mission statement at the center of our life? It is the difference between whether we live in the world we make or the world that others make for us. Without this kind of thinking, others will be happy to do our thinking for us. They will move their couch and their lamp into our living room, and we will sit down there.

My own personal mission statement—*I am made for Spiritual Nurture and for Public Capacity*—is now weathered and worn but it has helped me make choices in over thirty years of ministry. It reminds me that I am on this planet to nurture people as a pastor so that they have the capacity they need to bring peace and justice to the world. Because of this direction, I am able to make choices about what to do today and tomorrow. It let me choose the baptism for Friday and choose against another Bible study on the same day. Yes, I mess up all the time, for serendipity or for just plain laziness. But when I get on "top" of my preposterous, I find direction that definitely includes paying attention to the small. "The success of the intervention depends on the inner quality of the person doing the intervention." To stay well, I need spider webs.

In her new book called *Measuring a Life,* Dorothy Bass argues that the way most Americans measure our lives is by whether or not we are authentic (whatever that is). Whether or not we had free choice (whatever that is). Whether or not we made our own choices about who we are. I fear these versions of authenticity drip with individualism, like my favorite all-American character straight from the work of sociologist Robert Bellah who tells us "I am a self-made man," only to discover that he inherited the car dealership from his father. We are the victims of other people's creeds if we don't have our own. We become buried in a life that should bring us great joy. Pretty soon we are of no use to anyone.

We are not self-made. We are made by each other. In Thomas Friedman's new theory, one I happen to buy, the price of oil and the pace of freedom move in opposite directions. We are made by the price of oil as well as what we had for breakfast and what we learned in school and whether we were born Christians or not.

Having a measure for our lives, so that we know how to navigate the treacherous shoals of living well and doing good and keep them in balance, is a very simple, small strategy. Every one of us can do it. Some people—I think of many foundations and most school testing—take the notion of measurement too far, but on the other hand many of us don't take it far enough. How else would we know if our own lives, however long or short, measured up to goals we had set for ourselves? One goal could be to maximize serendipity. Another would be to leave a legacy of beauty or excellence or good jokes. A third would be to be a good parent or good school board member. Knowing our destination is a matter of creed, but also a matter of what furniture exists already in our living room. Is it cluttered with old stuff from our parents or our teachers or the oppressive voices that inhabit most of our minds? Interior decoration is not a small matter: once we have decided on it, we place small objects with love and honor.

My grandmother used to talk about having pins and needles all the time because she had poor circulation. This was long before acupuncture and its promise of healing by way of pins and needles. Our physical and spiritual retraining is a kind of spiritual acupuncture. Often we make decisions because we have experienced the tingle of fear: we aren't much interested in changing until something happens that says we need to change. We heard the doctor say our cancer was back or we heard the judge say the child would be convicted for using drugs or stealing computer data. We were put on full-body alert at the possibility that our pension was going to be taken away; we were so scared at how close we came to hitting the other car that we had to stop and rest a minute in order to experience our body's adrenaline rush. When we heard that our father lost his job after his heart bypass, fear got our full attention. When the fighting began in Lebanon, World War III crossed our minds. But we can also be drawn to the future with hope as well as pushed toward it by fear. We can retrain ourselves to take the initiative in a small way on behalf of large advances, personally and collectively.

Folk wisdom is right when it suggests that we put one foot in front of the other. Not both feet and not our whole body, but just one foot. In other words, we have to write the term paper one page at a time and we have to digest our meals one bite at a time. I often get so far ahead of myself that I forget to even enjoy where I am going! We are totalitarians when it comes to size. Getting to the right size and learning to appreciate the small are the twin engines of living well and doing good at the same time. Our wellness is threatened by totalitarianism; our good is threatened by the failure to imagine what large projects can be accomplished in small ways. When we place one foot in front of the other, we get somewhere. That "somewhere" has been our destination all along: the place where we can enjoy life, productively.

 CHAPTER NINE

SIMPLIFYING JOY

Joy is right under everything, right around every corner, and yet few of us ever make the trip "down" or "over." Instead, we are "surprised by joy," in that famous phrase of C. S. Lewis. Instead of joy being simple, it is elusive. Instead of being automatic, it seems to require effort. Instead being a given, joy seems to be something we have to get. When we simplify joy, we teach ourselves to expect it. We teach ourselves to assume it. We teach ourselves that it is a gift, all wrapped up on the table next to us. We give ourselves permission to open the day to joy—and to unwrap the gift as well.

A field of fireflies on a summer night can appear seemingly out of nowhere, reminding us to laugh. A child can find a cat hiding under a hassock, pretending no one can see him, and the child's discovery evokes giggles all around. A smile on the face of an old woman walking down the street can make us feel better. Saying "thank you" to the bus driver as we get off the bus can make us understand what Africans mean by "We greet each other." We notice each other. We remember with joy to have gratitude. Living well while doing good involves alertness to these flying fires as they pass by—and it can mean an active lighting of our lives with lightness and joy.

Simplifying joy may mean acting on it. Simplifying joy may mean coming to terms with how little joy there is. When I first came to Judson Memorial Church as pastor, I could tell that my "marching orders" were to clean up a variety of administrative messes. My other order—subliminal, of course—was not to turn us into an Uptown Church. We didn't want too much order, just enough to be able to find the mailing list, not enough to turn us into a corporation. I was amused by the instructions, most of the time. Then when I said there would no longer be smoking in the meeting room/sanctuary (welcome to Greenwich Village), there was a hue and cry: "We don't want to become an uptown church, we want to be open and free!" In the same set of decisions as a new leader, I supported a move to exclude pets in the meeting room/sanctuary, although it broke my heart. Why? We had a brand new rug. We had just spent $3 million on the room. Anyway, the very people who objected to these "rigidities" wrote a play, actually called a camp, which was performed at my installation. The choir sang with glee, "There's a puppy in the piano." I am still humming it. It was so much fun to manage the tension of these changes. How many more changes could be "finessed" by short operas?

In a nice restaurant one Sunday in Nice, France, a stately woman with very orange hair, orange suit, and orange shoes was seated at her table in the window, right next to her orange poodle. They shared a plate. Why does such a sight give us a simple joy? Because it is as absurd as people putting a puppy in the piano or smoking in the sanctuary. When things are absurd, we can laugh. We can laugh that laugh of acceptance and irony, the one that turns the page from tragedy to comedy.

Sometimes I think that joy is simply grace, realized. Grace is the undeserved gift of life; joy is when we know it. Grace, however, is a problem for many people. We just aren't quite sure about it. There is a great line in the third chapter of St. Paul's letter to the Romans where Paul asks about the relationship between sin and grace. To find our way to joy, we must get this relationship right. People who have the dual mission of living well while doing good must understand what the "good" really is. In this letter St. Paul is trying to rescue ethics from moralism when he playfully asks the question, "What, then, shall we sin more so that grace may abound?" (3:8). He sees the exhaustion of the ethical—not in the sense that bombs still destroy children and no one has the sense to use the word "ceasefire," but in the sense that trying to be good and do good results in a sinful self-righteousness. It is grace that makes us a good man or a good woman. Our own strivings do not. In a way the worst thing that could happen to an activist would be to be successful at changing the world. Then we really *would* be self-righteous. Instead, we are self-righteous in our efforts alone.

We can look at a woman all in orange feeding a dog expensive food as obnoxious, or we can look at it as funny. The choice is ours. We can realize and accept the reality in front of us—realize its grace—or we can complain about it.

Grace experienced is joy. Some people rush through dinner to get their second helping. Other people can't look up and see the fireflies in June. They see leaves turning brilliant colors and think of having to rake them; they see snow falling and think of shoveling. They miss seeing the sunsets in June and the bodaciousness of fall and the lace of winter snow. Such neglects are exactly what happen to us when our own goodness gets in the way of our good. We become stuck on being good, being right, being moral, changing the world—and the next thing we know all joy has fled. One of the verses of a great hymn "Dear Lord and Father of Mankind" asks God to "drop thy still dews of quietness, till all our strivings cease." It is in the moment when all our strivings cease that joy is created.

Sometimes I get the feeling that we who want to do good have moved into the Christian season of Lent and put our roots down. We have dug in. We "struggle" for justice, as I hear over and over in sermons or prayers, conversations, or meetings. Struggle is not a good strategy for the new world. Joy is the strategy. For me it is an Easter strategy, a dawn strategy, a peeking-over-the-horizon-and-winking-at-you strategy. That's why I insist on *both* living well and doing good. First we live well. First we get the hint that the tomb is empty. Then we do good out of deep responsiveness to the dawning light. Most people go the other way and argue that if we just do enough good, we can empty the tombs. Wrong direction. Theologically this error mimics the one we make when we live by works instead of grace: we think our work brings in the goodness. It does not. The good that we do comes from the grace we know. The more grace, the more joy, the more passion, the more virtue. That is the direction, theologically and practically. Otherwise we are just trying to bring in the good on our own. We are working too hard at what is not work.

We can be sure that if we can get out of our own way, joy will move into our spiritual house. We can wait on it, as the psalmist says: "Weeping may linger for the night, but joy comes with the morning" (Ps. 30:5). How do we evacuate the tombs? It is not by working hard at justice; it is by realizing that justice will come. The grace of justice will follow, like morning follows day.

One parishioner of mine showed me this truth about joy. Her doctor had just told this octogenarian that she had very little time left to live, and she came to see me. Her visit was ostensibly about her imminent funeral, to tell me how she wanted it, and to air a burden about an adult child of hers who was in deep trouble. But she really wanted to tell me about the painted buntings—those small, colorful birds that migrate to Florida during the fall, which is actually Florida's spring. Characteristically, she began with an apology: "I don't know if I should tell you because you are so busy, and you have to sit still for a long time, in the right place, to see the buntings."

A few days after the visit, she called with genuine enthusiasm in her voice and announced: "The painted buntings have returned!" The message was also more deeply coded. I had chided her during her earlier visit about her silence about herself, her chatter about her daughter. I had tried to suggest it was time to think about herself. She needed to live well after a long life of doing good. When she told me about the birds and her delight in them, she was letting me know who she is: she is a woman capable of delight in small things. She knows joy despite life-long burden and sorrow. She knows how to see the big in the little.

I, who talk about myself at the drop of a hat, have few regrets compared to hers. And conceivably less joy as well. I don't always know how to sit still long enough for the return of the buntings. I have missed more than one spring; my friend has not. She knows how to look deeply enough to see simple delight, the joy of seasons changing.

Why do we mourn the death of a Palestinian adolescent whose face is blown off by an Israeli soldier? Or vice versa? Because we mourn the springs the boy and the soldier will miss. The returning buntings that they no longer will get to see. The little things stolen from them both by the so-called big things. Why do we get chills at a car crash, mourn a low-income apartment building wiped out in a nameless flood? Because we don't see the strangers who did stop as we passed by, the manager who took in the dog of one of the residents. He didn't have to take in her dog. He could have stayed aloof—and missed the buntings, ignored the spring, been defeated by the mountain of trouble that the little birds fly over and seed with joy.

Right now one of my parishioners has taken in the dog of another who is in jail. The dog is a pain in the neck—and still the woman befriending the dog finds joy in it. This same dog was the occasion for the song about the puppy in the piano. My congregation amazes me with the way they can turn difficult problems—a jailed parishioner, a dog that needs care, a new rug to keep clean—into fun. They simplify to joy. I don't know that it took any effort at all to find a home for the dog because three people lined up to volunteer, including a mother of two grown daughters whose husband vetoed her generosity.

The whole matter of who would take the dog became a light burden. No one complained. People just lifted. The one who got lucky enough to have the dog (as she sees it) has learned the trick of finding the joy that is under the hassock in the deep foundation of life. She has learned the trick of grace realized. Many people would say that the dog of a criminal should be put to sleep. She would never think that. She lives on the other side of being good. She is not too good for her own good. She is better than that.

As some people miss every train they should have caught, most of the life they should have lived, other people pause. Other people pay attention. Other people notice that they are alive and are glad.

Sometimes the people who notice the most are the people with the most distractions in their lives—and not the usual distraction of "I'm just so busy!" but the universal condition of dolor, suffering, genuine first-class trouble. People with brain tumors stop by and talk about how hard it is to wait for the next MRI. I press them: "How will you manage?"

"Fly fishing," they announce. If people on the edge of the grave can notice the return of the buntings, so can those of us a few feet away.

If the first strategy is to pay deep attention to life and what is still living in us, and the second is to take care of someone else's dog or something else "inconvenient," then the third is to mimic God in graceful behavior. My English teacher in college did just that.

It was 1969 and I had been involved in "student power" and "anti-war" demonstrations for most of my four years in college. I was supposed to graduate in 1969, and I did, but surely by no merit of my own. You could call it a lucky break that my senior advisor let me graduate without having my work done. But you could also call it grace, that thing that simplifies effort and allows you to dive for deeper meaning. In 1969 I couldn't make myself do a senior English thesis. As I saw it the world was exploding outside my door and while Sinclair Lewis was interesting, the world was more so. My professor did not even agree with the politics of student power, but he did know what it meant to pay attention to the world and its largeness. When I told him I couldn't do it, he just smiled. "I'll put in a good grade, you do it over the summer, and you will graduate. I will trust you." Trust is a form of joy just as grace is. I have had many occasions as a teacher to pass on and pay back this little grace. There are lots of things wrong with deadlines, including their language; often what a students need is a lifeline. They need a teacher who understands there is life outside the door: the fireflies may have arrived, and we can't just work all the time.

I've said that my congregation wanted me to "clean up" the place without destroying its sense of humor, which is exactly why I wanted to be their minister. They had the proper balance between work and joy. I'm not sure I did— or do. I still go nuts when dozens of newsletter are returned because the address isn't right or people praise the grunge of the gym and the "good old days." I did enjoy, at least once, using my freedom to hire an "iffy" candidate—the woman who told me on the phone about her pink hair required at least a look. She proved to be an extremely impressive, well-organized, shoeless Baptist converting to Judaism. She gives me joy. She returns some of the painted buntings that the winter of aging and organization took away from me.

The bridge between letting trust and grace and joy be while still looking for them is in the verb *enchantment.* To allow life to enchant us. I can tell you all I know about enchant-ment by telling you about my best friend, the Hudson River. One of the best things an activist can do is to develop low-cost personal pleasures. The river rarely costs me anything. But from it I draw enormous power. Is this power and pleas-ure small or large? It is both.

Let me start with the other river, the one to which I can walk in fifteen minutes from my East Side apartment. On an NPR story recently, a woman read a poem called "I am the East River." She began, "I am NOT the storied, bridged, statued Hudson. Instead I am the East River: without me Manhattan would just be Queens." I feel the same way about the Hudson River; without it I would just be Kingston, New York. Instead, I have found my way into a great geography. I never say I grew up upstate because peo-ple snicker, so instead I say I grew up on the Hudson. That gets their attention. Instead of being someone from an armpit like Queens or Kingston, I am someone from somewhere. I come from one of the spines of the world. I remember not realizing that Kingston meant a degraded, abandoned factory town to most people when I first got to college, a minor miracle all by itself. People would snicker—and start talking about where they came from. Lancaster, Syracuse, Long Island, Montclair, places with a better pedigree. Until I saw Kingston through their eyes, I had no idea it was ugly, because where I came from—the river—it was stunningly beautiful. Because of it, I defined myself as beautiful. I had no idea that I came down from a Tannersville family of horse stealers to be the first child of a man who couldn't hold a job, and if he did, he spent the whole paycheck on beer for the softball team. The Hudson kept me from looking at all that and demanded that I look at it.

Without the Hudson I could neither live well nor do good. Because of the Hudson, I am able to think of my own smallness in large ways. I am able to take a small, inexpensive pleasure and turn it into something lofty like enchantment. I see her blue or grey, dark or clear, seasoned or seasonless. We have been best friends since I was a kid growing up on the wrong side of a town that the garment industry abandoned. I ice skated on Dinky's pond, a tributary to the great river, and sometimes if the water was cold enough long enough, without snow, I could skate along a twig-cluttered finger all the way to a river view. The pond was dinky, but only in the sense that it was small. Moons rose over it. Stars lit the ice skater's way. A fire burned in the skate house. Boys chased you on the ice, with scarves flying. You forgot to be cold. You realized joy. You experienced grace. You trusted the thin ice to hold you up.

Winter was just the appetizer for the summer. Then, I moved "downtown" to the Point, the name we who had not much else called our river spa. There I swam and swam until eventually some intrusive adult would scoop me up, dry me off, and take me to a place they called home but I did not.

My home was in the joy of floating in my river. The Hudson received me without comment. She accepted me, skinny butt and all.

I never see her without that girlish thrill, even today from Manhattan's East Village where 1.4 miles later I can be close to tugs and barges, hawks and shad, the river's emptying into the big sea. I know about the PCBs in the shad and that even with all the protein in the river, the blue crabs are about all you can eat. I know how bad things got for the Hudson, how it became yellow and green instead of blue and grey. I have also learned that things can change; now you can swim in it again. The river is my best friend because of its longer, deeper, wider life rhythms. There is the iridescence of a twenty-two-inch shad, the great blue heron who always acts like she owns the place. Last week as the shad began to run a fisherman was interviewed on NPR. The reporter asked, "Why care about the shad?" He responded, "Is there anything else to care about?" I know how he feels, especially when I found myself at Grand Central Station several days after we first moved to the city, buying a ticket just to ride the train to Poughkeepsie and then ride back. I even bought a second ticket to take the Amtrak the next leg on up to Rhinecliff. There I had lunch and went back. I get deeply purposeless when I get around the Hudson. It has enough purpose for both of us.

How can people who have to save the world realize joy? Skip out every now and then. Call in "well." Take a train ride. Go ice skating. Go swimming. Get your face out of the screen, off the email, and look out the window. Why do many of us feel nervous about being away from our computers? Because we allow work and connection to define us. Joy is giving play permission to define us. I love to put a message on my machine that says, "Limited connectivity through Tuesday." What I really mean is I am disconnecting with the computer and connecting to the river, or the sun, or the book. I am not just disconnecting. I am also reconnecting.

We are pulled by grace into joy, by joy into justice. When I say we are pulled into a good future, where another world is possible, what I mean is that we don't push the barge upriver. We are pulled, we do not push. We are pulled by our small capacity to have small pleasures, to connect ourselves to the things that roll by us right outside our door. Your *kazen* may not be a river, or a spider web. It may be a tree or a stream, a rock or a road, a street or a painting. It is a sacred place, a *sanctum sanctorum*. Some people think swamps are sacred places. The point is to have one and to live in it in a holy way.

What I care about in the river is its sensuality, what it is to my eyes, when a dusk pink can take its blue and create glisten. I care about what it is to my body when I swim and water hits skin and takes away the sense of having to haul my own weight around. I care about the way it takes the work out of me and calms my fear about who or what is going to die next. I care about the way a tugboat makes me giggle. Why? Because the games my sister and brother and I played in the water at the Point in Kingston were these: "Do you want to be the tug or the barge? No, it's my turn to be the tug. You've been the tug for too long. Mommy, tell her it is my turn to be the tug."

Pleasure is the place we start; the pleasure we take in small, nearby things is the pleasure that grounds us for larger challenges. This grounding becomes enchantment, enchantment with the way the world is. From there we may dare to try to change it.

Sigmund Freud termed these small experiences of horizon or nature "oceanic," and it has been a hallmark of religious mysticism in virtually every tradition one can think of.

A good deal of spiritual practice, from long periods of meditation to extended fasting to intense prayer, has as its goal a lessening of our sense of separation, of rigid demarcation between "me" and the rest of creation. When I swam as a child I had this experience, day in and day out. Once the boundary between inner life (living well) and outer life (doing good) dissolves, we are prepared for the exuberance and froth and fullness of it all. Glee is the glue between living well and doing good.

Joy is realized grace. It is right outside your window. It is right down the street and under the hassock. It is sneaking around in your next decision. It is being enchanted by the preposterous pile on your desk. It is a painted bunting with orange and pink hair, and it may even be true that there are puppies in the piano. Joy is a lifeline to living well enough to do good.

 CHAPTER 10

HOW TO LIVE WELL
AND DO GOOD

L iving well and doing good is a matter of becoming "salubrious." This is my new favorite word—I like its ebullience. To be salubrious is to be so healthy that we overflow in service, so well that we overflow in wellness and assist the world around us in being well. "Salut!" is the toast many use over a glass of wine. It means, "To your health!" Salubrious means to your health and the health of us all.

In this book I have tried to hold the self and the world together in one salubrious knot. We act for the world's health from our own health; the world's health becomes our health as well. It takes a village for a person to be well and it takes well people for villages to be well. This cycle and flow is like a fountain, water shot into the beautiful air, inner and outer strength.

Oddly, all this light has its foundation in darkness. The first turn in the knot of living well and doing good is to humanize ourselves. The Sufi poet Rumi said: "Be kind to everyone you meet. Everyone you meet is carrying a burden of some kind." Everyone. You. Me. Us. Them. When you know it is good to be kind because everyone is carrying a burden, you melt a little. Soft is good. Soft is to hard as compassion is to conceit.

Marianne Williamson, the very popular New Age guru, whom usually I like to demonize, supposedly said, "The real shadow in America is that it thinks it has no shadow." Ah. The real shadow is shadowlessness. The real shadow is not seeing the burden that all of us—war proponents or war foes, Republicans or Democrats, Israelis or Palestinians—are carrying. Those of us who oppose the war often dehumanize those who promote the war, and thus we enter the dehumanization project. This is the real shadow. We have no enemies but ourselves. Living well and doing good begins in the recognition of our shadow and our burden.

I love a story a friend just told me about her sister growing up in a small Oregon town. She was talking about one of her son's friends, a boy who was on probation from school because he had been caught drunk. One more offense and he would be out. She was comparing his experience with something in her own past. As a girl in 1959 she was pulled over for driving with a beer in her hand in this small town. She was so upset when the policeman stopped her that she threw the beer can out the window, in full sight of the cop. He charged her with littering. We have to help each other along and cut each other some slack. We become aware that we are gifted and burdened, burdened and gifted. We are mixed-up people still who hope to live well and do good.

Fundamentally we think small and ordinary is the route to large and important. We are joyful about how the small carries the large and the ordinary carries the sacred. We spend most of our attention on incarnational thinking during the Christmas season. Many complain about how commercial Christmas has become: "The decorations are up too early...The Play Station Threes have created mass consumeristic hysteria...Let's get the Christ back in Xmas." These laments miss the point of Christmas because Christmas is about commerce. It is about the ordinary carrying the holy. The carols all sing about a God from heaven to earth come down. Getting the Christ back in Christmas is not something we do in church, but something we can also do at the mall. Imagine that: holy behavior in public worlds, holy living in living rooms and kitchens, holy living in boardrooms and Congress. That is what the incarnation means. *Encarnacion*. Christ *con carne*. Christ in the meat. God is in the meat of things.

So the next time someone gripes about the commercialization of Christmas, tell them about the incarnation. Tell them how beautiful the mall was meant to be—and tell them about the peace and justice that was intended for the world too. "Merry Christmas" means "Merry Ordinary Holy World." We who try to live well and do good live Christmas all year long.

I have to conclude this book of hope with some fear. I write on the second day of the new year of 2007, aware that I am a gardener and that I always worry. I worry if it is too cold or too hot. I worry if there is too much rain and not enough. Gardeners worry. We molly-coddle our plants, the way an inexperienced mother overdoes her baby's bath. Often our worry is useless; our plants thrive, with or without our fears for their safety.

Nevertheless, I saw forsythia about to burst in Forty Tryon Park on December 23. On December 31 I saw cherry blossoms budding in Sag Harbor, and on the same day, daffodils in Easthampton. In November I hiked an afternoon in the Shawganuck Mountains, near New Paltz. I came back covered in ticks. Why? It was too warm. My cats have had a great holiday: nonstop mice whose little heads they can bite off. Why? The mice, and surely the local rats too, love the phony autumn. Last night I watched the premature courage of daffodils in Stuyvesant Park: I wanted to push them down so they would be safe from January. Instead I stood there and worried.

My worry is new: it is not the same old worry. The reason is that it is not the same old world. Gardeners join scientists in not having to worry that the diagnosis of global warming is correct. Its evidence is spring in autumn and winter, ticks and mice who are happily confused. Its evidence is at Bloomingdales where winter coats are still on racks and in buds that bloom too soon. The only thing left for gardeners and scientists to discuss is how soon the gardens we know will be destroyed. The issue is not if, but when.

How dare we live well when there is not just good to be done but evil to stop? What is a gardener to do if spring has already come and it's just January? Here we are with iris six inches high and daffodils courageously busting through soft ground in January. What are we to do?

Do not try to push the daffodils down into the ground: the call of the warmth is stronger than any dirt. They will reassert themselves. If the daffodil hears the call of warmth, it will push through. Will the flowers be any good if the proper dormancy has not been achieved? Probably not, but that will be just one of many ways global warming will wound us.

Do cover the iris over with a Christmas tree or two. They will like the protection and the acid of the decaying needles. The tree will not hurt them if properly placed. That will also make you think you are doing something to save the spring that never, by the way, is normal. It's always bad in some way or another—too late, too early, too wet, too dry. Be careful of normalizing spring. And still and nonetheless, take action to keep spring properly abnormal.

Do plant mesclun. My arugula in the city is doing fine. We had some for Thanksgiving and I doubly enjoyed its bitter taste.

Do cut forsythia and bring it into the house to "force" it. It will give you the fantasy that you are in the tropics and also engage all your guests in tragic talk. We need the tragedy: otherwise we will say silly things like, "If this is our fate and our future, let us lie back and enjoy it." If one more person says that to me, I will steal her coat. Pretty soon she won't even need it.

On the more spiritual side, I continue my ordinary, every two-hour piece of advice to myself in the gardening context: Don't worry. Be happy. Worry gets you nowhere at all. Anger causes change. Do not say that nothing can be done. Remember that very little has even been tried. In New York, we campaign to close off every other street and tax cars coming into the city. Some of us bike on Friday night at seven o'clock from Union Square while the police chase us instead of the cars. Another suggestion is to raise the price of gas to $4 per gallon immediately. Think what that will do to traffic on our highways, not to mention the Long Island Railroad and the Hampton Jitney. People love to say that anything that bans cars is impractical. They haven't seen how much money the auto industry paid in advertising to make the Kyoto Accord appear foolish. What is impractical is spring in winter, not banning cars.

Finally, don't be afraid of fear. Fear, anger, and visionary action will save spring from winter. Be afraid when you walk in Fort Tryon Park before Christmas and see blooming forsythia and picnickers on the lawn. Fear them. They forecast spiritual, economic, social, and environmental crisis. These things are worth being afraid for.

A beautiful story is recounted every Christmas in the forests of Provence in southern France. It's about the four shepherds who came to Bethlehem to see the child. One brought eggs, another bread and cheese, the third brought wine, and the fourth brought nothing at all. People called him L'Enchante. The first three shepherds chatted with Mary and Joseph, commenting on how well Mary looked, how cozy the cave, and how handsome Joseph was. Finally someone asked, "Where is L'Enchante?" They searched high and low, and finally someone peeked through the blanket hung up against the crib into the crèche. There kneeling at the crib was L'Enchante, who stayed the entire night in adoration. Another response, beyond silence and action, to the call from the wild is enchantment. Simple enchantment.

The Leave It Alone committee needs more work. You and I don't. We do a little and leave it to the pine needles to help the iris along.

The writer William Miller, in his book *The Mystery of Courage*, argues that a new kind of courage is needed, the courage to come out of our cocoon. Consider a normal evening. We come home from work, frazzled and spent. We walk into our kitchens and are not surprised that our partner and kids are not home. We take what we like most out of our refrigerators and put it in the microwave and stare at the paper on the kitchen table. Let's say it is Wednesday and our favorite television show is on, followed by a game of the home team. Our pulse quickens a little. The show is good, our partner comes home, we exchange a few words, we find the game boring, and so we move to the den to write an overdue memo on our computer. First we check our email and the latest news, then play a computer game. We say goodnight to our spouse and go to bed.

Is this, asks Miller, a "Christian" evening? We have not coveted our neighbor's spouse, stolen anything, or ordered anyone around. We have enjoyed moments of a pleasant, well-fed freedom—eating what we liked, watching what we liked, and doing what we liked. Miller argues that, indeed, this is what most people around the world want also: a safe, quiet cocoon. The same freedom to do next to nothing while getting three squares a day.

But we are still surrounded by the possibility of something better. Here on the shelf is the poetry we could read to each other. There in the corner are the flute and the guitar we could play together. Right next to the kitchen is an underused dining room table. Not far from our home are the playing fields where we could teach our sons and daughters tennis and join a softball league with our beloved. Within easy reach are the museums where local painters show their work and the concert hall where the citizens' symphony plays. There are also meetings where activists struggle to find the patriotic way to peace.

Many radicals argue that devotion to family and communal celebrations seem bland and retrograde goals, better than consumption and shopping but not exactly the stuff of bold designs and revolutionary politics. Where are your big dreams? Of course, they include peace. They include rice for Afghani children. They include women at the table. And all these dreams may require something from you—not five $100 bills so much as ways to find the courage to cross the threshold from the TV room to the dining room, the home to the community. There are other thresholds to cross. We need to move out of the room of unencumbered personal freedom into a world that has a lineage, a legacy, a past—and therefore a future.

Americans have an awesome freedom to cocoon; the question right now is whether we should be using it or whether, instead, we should be booking a passage to somewhere larger than our family room. Living well while doing good is cocoon, plus.

Simplifiers keep an inner fire lit while avoiding burnout in the larger world. I like to remember the many different scriptures about fire, particularly the one Jeremiah used to describe himself when he said he had "a burning fire shut up in my bones" (Jeremiah 20:9). Most of us have a fire shut up in our bones because we just don't know how to do everything and therefore we often do nothing. The simplifier strategy is to do something and to let the rest be.

There are a lot of mixed messages in scripture about fire. The prophet Isaiah tells us that God will not quench even "a dimly burning wick" (42:3). Shadrach, Meshach, and Abednego were cast into the fire, yet God protected them from the flames (Daniel 3:27). The disciples who walked the road to Emmaus with the risen Jesus asked, "Did not our hearts burn within us while he talked to us on the road?" (Luke 24:32). When their hearts were strangely warmed, surely the experience was not just simplifying. It was probably also challenging. It meant something was expected of them. They were in a warm *and* fiery pit. One associate pastor said of the senior pastor, ten years her junior, "He just hasn't been through anything yet." She was talking about the fiery pit of raising four children on her own. Many of us are so overwhelmed by the demands of our cocoon that we can't imagine going "out" and going through something.

I was once in a nursing home visiting a patient and had to walk through the room where everyone was taking the afternoon sun. A woman I knew by sight had squashed her Wonder Bread sandwich into a ball and was staring at it with lively amazement. She stopped as I ran by, not wanting to get involved in the Wonder Bread compression, and looked me straight in the eye: "What do you think they want me to do with this?" I said, knowing I was trapped, "I think they want you to eat it." She stopped mauling the bread and said, "You've got to be kidding."

I often pray in her words: "God, what do you want me to do with this?" My response is often, "You've got to be kidding!" But I want to leave you on a note of hope—not that you *should* hope, but that you *may* hope. Here are the nine principles that have guided me as I have tried to learn how to live well while doing good.

1. Resist moralism
Imagine writing a woman whose husband has been murdered by a policeman and saying, "You should have hope." Or telling a woman who has to work and raise four children on her own, "Let me offer some inspirational scriptures to make you feel bad about your despair." I don't think so.

2. Don't keep your bulletproof vest on too long
One way we manage despair is to defend ourselves against it. It takes courage to believe things can be better. Amelia Earhart said, "Courage is the price life exacts for peace." There will be no peace until there is justice.

3. Use tricks

I know many of us say, "I'll never find someone to love or who will love me," but for just today act as if you're wrong. Be charming and available—at least until after dinner.

4. Consider the alternatives

In the last episode of the television series "Mash," Corporal Klinger realizes that he has two choices: to stop loving and stay safe, or to keep loving and be in constant danger. If he shuts his heart down it may feel good for a while, but then he has to live into a long life without love. Consider what doors bang close if you don't eat your despair.

5. Stay at the table

Don't leave in disgust. Hang on to your seat. Let the others leave the church, the nation, and the job. Be people who last. Be obnoxious and persist.

6. Be real

Build communities of people who are willing to look at their own despair. Speak often and openly about your shadow.

7. Don't do everything

Do something. Write one letter to your congressman if you can't organize a whole demonstration. Make it a good letter.

8. Be generous

Care about somebody you don't have to care about. Even if it is just one person.

9. Rename yourself

When I have had it with everybody and everything and I want to scream at the whole world, "What do you want me to do with this?" I take a suggestion from Emily Dickinson and rename myself "feathers." "Hope is a thing with feathers." Hope is the broken body of a good man at table with his friends, on the night when he was betrayed. Samuel Langhorne Clemens renamed himself Mark Twain from his riverboat experience. The phrase "mark twain" means two fathoms deep, which for a riverboat captain is just deep enough water to navigate. Go deep enough to navigate, then stay at table and eat what is there. Salut.